# Gudrun's Kitchen

## RECIPES FROM A NORWEGIAN FAMILY

Ingeborg Hydle Baugh
Irene O. Sandvold
Edward O. Sandvold
Quinn E. Sandvold

Wisconsin Historical Society Press

Published by the Wisconsin Historical Society Press
*Publishers since 1855*
© 2011 by the State Historical Society of Wisconsin

wisconsin**history**.org

Photographs and illustrations are from the authors' collections unless otherwise credited. Front cover photos: [top] © Punchstock, [bottom] © iStockPhoto / ALEAIMAGE.

Printed in Wisconsin, U.S.A.
Designed by Andrew J. Brozyna, ajbdesign.com

15 14 13 12 11    1 2 3 4 5

Library of Congress Cataloging-in-Publication Data

Baugh, Ingeborg Hydle.
Gudrun's kitchen: recipes from a Norwegian family/Ingeborg Hydle Baugh . . . [et al.].
    p. cm.
Includes bibliographical references and index.
ISBN 978-0-87020-462-3 (pbk. : alk. paper) 1. Sandvold, Gudrun Thue, b. 1902.
2. Sandvold, Gudrun Thue, b. 1902—Family. 3. Norwegian Americans—Wisconsin—Biography. 4. Norwegian Americans—Cultural assimilation—Wisconsin. 5. Fort Atkinson (Wis.)—Biography. 6. Cooking, Norwegian. 7. Cooking—Wisconsin. I. Title.
F590.S2B38 2011
641.59775—dc22
                        2011004314

*To Gudrun Thue Sandvold, Irving Sandvold, and Eddie Sandvold.*
*Your love lives on in all of us.*

Gudrun in Chicago before her marriage

# CONTENTS

# Preface

This is the story of a life in food and family. Gudrun's children grew up in a home that never lacked for love or good food, and this book is their collaboration. Siblings Edward and Irene Sandvold planned this cookbook over many years, collecting recipes, reminiscing, and working little by little to capture not only the taste of Gudrun's cooking but also the heart that she put into it. When Eddie passed away in 2005, Irene felt an urgency to preserve her mother's and brother's legacies for her own children and future generations. To complete the project, she sought the help of Eddie's son Quinn and her own daughter, Ingeborg. Ingeborg, who was only a toddler when her grandmother died, took on the task of researching our family's life in Norway and arrival in the United States, where our story is one in the tapestry of American history. Ingeborg then conducted family interviews, collected stories, transferred our oral history into writing, and compared the oral tradition to the various documents and records she uncovered in her genealogical research. Finally, the three authors tested recipes to their hearts' delight and compiled what we believe is an exhaustive collection of Gudrun's recipes as written by Irene and Eddie while their mother was cooking. Gudrun always said her main ingredient was tender loving care.

# PART I
## The Gudrun Chronicles
ADVENTURE, ROMANCE, FAMILY, AND FOOD

The Digital Archives/ National Archives of Norway

| Nr. | Fødsels-Datum | Daabsdatum (opgaa the Hjemmedøbte) | For Hjemme-døbte: Daabs-Stadfæstelsens Datum | Barnets fulde Navn | Forældrenes fulde Navne og borgerlige Stilling (Næringsvei) | Forældrenes Bopæl | Forældrenes Fødselsaar (Faderen / Moderen) | | Fadderes Navne og borgerlige Stilling |
|---|---|---|---|---|---|---|---|---|---|
| 11 | 13.5 | 22.6 | | Anna Birte Marie | g. Anders Gregoriussen Strand, Vendel Marie | Olode - Strand | 1839 | 1852 | Søinct H. Hindenes; Martha H. Liltaa; Guth H. Strand; Pernille P. Myklebust, Andreas A. Johansen, Chann H. Strand. |
| 12 | 28.4 | 22.6 | | Margit Johanna | Nadmit Ola Hansen Raaø, Marie Anders | Aakesunds | 1876 | 1878 | Hanne Klaus H. Raaø; Anders Olsen hielsen; Gjerhard A. Lillaa, Oskine J. de Julie H. A-; Amalie A. Raaø. |
| 13 | 3.6 | 6.7 | | Astrid Inga Marie | g. Inus Andersson Halse, Sirin Tostedts | Halse | 1878 | 1878 | g. Martinus M. Sundal; Guttorm Simonsen Jan Baane; H. Anna A. Sundal; Haroline A. de; g. Halse P. Skovid. |
| 14 | 11.4 | 4.7 | | Juliane | Oanbruger Andreas Jakobsen Lindberg g. Ommep...ge Josepine Johannsdtr Palen | Uden Ægteskab | ? | 1876 | Constr...ge: aimani Karl Ludriksen Rovmten, hus. Juliande; - Ob B. Jgrolsen g. Austri Mellen Jør. |
| 15 | **15.6** | 20.7 | | Marta Sofie | g. Jakob Mikkelsen Ækrem, Birte Olet | Ækrem | 1845 | 1852 | g. Kristen M. Ækrem; g. Søinct K. Kr.; Anders g. do.; Lisa Pl. Ækrem; Karen Olsdtr Ækrem. |
| 16 | 2.5 | 20.7 | | Gjudrun | Bottolf Helgesen Thue, Larr, Ingeborg Andersdtr. | Aaem | 1856 | 1868 | Landh. Bent. Bøe; Mahen Bøe; Guynnnd L. Apelsten; Sni Dona Zelstrn; Lh. J. Palse; Marie P. Johannsane. |
| 17 | 14.7 | 31.8 | | Inga Johanna | g.h. Johan Olsen Morsstad/ Johanne Olaijso Osane | Morsat | 1875 | 1875 | Stor. Karles Osane; Hs. Olar O. Frie; Ingebon Osane; Johanne gb Morsatt; Johanne O. Saul | 
| 18 | 2.5 | 25.9 | | Alette Sofie Borgithe | g. Anna Olassen; Josepina Danielsdtt | Gjusdal | 1855 | 1840 | Peder S. Biirkd; Jno M. Pirula; Lars O. Frie; Anne A. Frie; Marta L. Haivum; Marte P. gjusdal. |

Gudrun's baptism record, 1902. Gudrun is Number 16.

This is the story of Gudrun Thue Sandvold. The youngest of a large Norwegian family, she was known for her beaming blue eyes and a reserve that gave way to laughter whenever she got together with her sisters. She took immeasurable pride in her children and grandchildren, scouting garage sales for little treasures for her grandsons and sending care packages all over the world to her well-traveled daughter, Irene. She kept an exquisite home, decorating her Christmas tree as if it would adorn the White House, and she turned the most mundane occasion into a party. She delighted in caring for people, especially her husband, Irving. And to all who knew her, Gudrun's cooking was the stuff of legend.

In the tiny Norwegian village of Åheim[1], on a farm of the same name, not far from Nordfjord's sparkling glaciers, far-reaching inlets, and narrow valleys, Ingeborg Maurstad Thue (too-ē) at age forty-four gave birth to her last child on May 2, 1902.[2] Ingeborg and

---

1. This would have been spelled Aahjem at the time, as it was on Gudrun's passport.

2. Gudrun's sister Synva always contended there were fifteen siblings. To date, our memories and research in church records have uncovered only eleven siblings, including one, Bård, who died in infancy. Gudrun always said she was the thirteenth and youngest child in the family. Perry's children, Little Borghild, Little Gudrun, and Little Perry and a cousin, Sigurd Thue, also lived in Gudrun's home during her childhood.

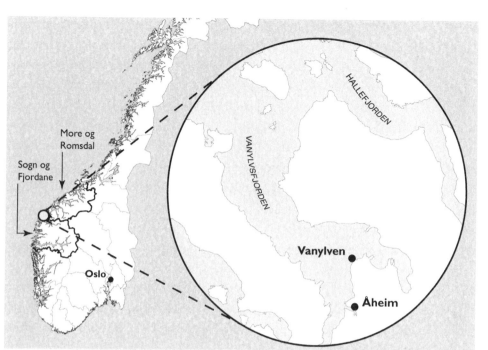

Joel Heiman

her husband, Bottolf, a teacher, named their new baby girl Gudrun, an Old Norse name meaning "God's mystery."[3]

Her oldest brother, Helge, was over twenty years her senior. He was followed by several brothers and sisters: Peder (nicknamed Perry), Synneve (called Synva), Martha, Astrid, Ingeborg, Bård (named for a brother who died only months before Bård was born), Ragnhild, Borghild, and Gudrun. Between 1897 and 1909, all but four siblings immigrated to America one by one and settled in the Midwest, leaving behind only Ingeborg, Bård, Borghild, and Gudrun. Eventually, only Ingeborg and Bård would remain in Norway.

Gudrun was born during a time of great change for her family and for Norway. The migration of her family was not unlike that of many Norwegians who sailed the Atlantic for the United States. Farmers were drawn to America's promise of land, urban workers

---

3. Also "God's secret lore" or "God's wisdom."

sought higher wages, and adventurers joined relatives who had come before them, draining Norway's shores of human capital throughout the nineteenth century and into the early twentieth century. In fact, during the migration, Norway lost a greater proportion of its citizens to America than any country except Ireland—about 800,000 people, or a third of the population, between 1820 and 1920—a fact that would forever tie the two nations as if they were cousins themselves. Yet the Thue family's immigration story is also atypical: while the first waves of European immigrants came to America mainly to escape lives of poverty and tyranny, and the majority of these settled in rural areas, Gudrun and her siblings came slightly later, lured by the experiences reported by family members who came before them, and most of them made new, relatively prosperous lives for themselves in cities.

The social and political trends taking shape in Norway and Western Europe during the nineteenth and twentieth centuries paralleled what was occurring in America: the establishment of liberal institutions, a progressive social trajectory, and rapid industrialization. After being on the losing side of the Napoleonic Wars, following four hundred years under Danish rule, Norway had been ceded to Sweden in 1814. However, in the midst of this transition, Norway declared its independence and adopted a liberal constitution in the American and French models on May 17, 1814, the Norwegian National Day exuberantly celebrated by Norwegians the world over as Syttende Mai. On November 4 Norway forged a union with Sweden as an independent kingdom under the Swedish monarch, retaining its own constitution and institutions.

Over the next hundred years, Norwegians sought to define and express a distinct national character, which celebrated the folk traditions of the rural peasantry. This period of cultural rebirth produced world-renowned authors, musicians, and artists, most notably writers Henrik Ibsen and Bjørnstjerne Bjørnson and composer Edvard Grieg. Spurred by this strengthening nationalism and dissatisfaction with Sweden's foreign policies, Norway unilaterally dissolved the union and achieved a peaceful separation from Sweden on June 7, 1905. To this day, Norway fiercely guards its independence and sovereignty, exemplified by its repeated refusal to join the European Union.

The twentieth century also brought with it a new phase of industrialization. With the power of waterfalls harnessed, factories began using electricity. New roads and railway, steamer, postal, and telegraphic services linked the different parts of the country, which heretofore had been largely secluded from one another. And so Norway emerged as an urban-industrial society with a distinct independent and egalitarian national identity and a progressive cultural and social direction.

For the Thue clan, the end of the nineteenth century brought its own changes, primarily the family's own one-by-one migration to America. The migration was largely driven by relatives who had preceded them, starting with Gudrun's pioneering paternal uncle, Helge H. Thue, and her maternal uncle John P. Maurstad, who sailed to America in 1881. Helge eventually settled in Horace, North Dakota, just south of Fargo, where in 1890 he married Caroline Brink and the same year went into the mercantile business with his father-in-law, Hans Christian Olson Brink.[4]

The first of Gudrun's siblings to join their Uncle Helge was her oldest brother, also named Helge, in 1897. He worked briefly at a farm near Horace and then went to school and clerked in the Twin Cities. He served five years in the military and moved west to Seattle. He lost touch with his family in America and only reunited with them when he returned to Horace shortly before his death in 1935.

Helge was followed by Martha in 1902 and Perry in 1903, who both initially settled in Waukegan, Illinois, where some of their cousins already resided. Perry died of typhoid fever there at age thirty, and his widow, Anna Farstad, temporarily returned to Norway with Little Borghild, Little Gudrun, and Little Perry, who grew up alongside Gudrun as her contemporaries. (Using the "little" prefix was the only way to distinguish among the multiple Borghilds and Gudruns in the household.)

There is scant information about Perry's life and experience of traveling to America, but Martha's late daughter, Liv "Tuty" (Brakke) Hertsgaard, who lived to be ninety-seven years old, told her mother's story in a conversation with Ingeborg Hydle Baugh in 2007.

---

4. Uncle Helge's father-in-law, Hans Christian Olson Brink, had moved from Norway to Minnesota in 1867, where he began life on new soil as a farmhand, then acquired his own land under the Homestead Act of 1862, and eventually amassed 412 acres. Although several of the Thue siblings from Norway worked on a farm near Horace, North Dakota, upon their arrival in America, there is no evidence that their uncle Helge Thue owned farmland. It seems likely that they were given work at the Brink farm, perhaps as a way to pay back the cost of their ship passage.

At age seven, Martha was sent to live with her *Moster* Vediche and her husband, John Myklebust, in the nearby village of Eid.[5] There she was charged with caring for the younger Myklebust children, who were nearly her age. Several of the older Myklebust children had taken the journey to America before the turn of the century, and by the age of fourteen Martha was keen to go next, but her father urged her to wait until her cousins had settled in. Finally, she made the trip at age seventeen. Tuty described her mother's excitement and trepidation during the two-week transatlantic trip:

> When she got to England the first night of her voyage, she stood at the railing under the big sky full of stars and thought, 'What have I done?' and she started to cry. Her travel companion, Isak Faleide [their cousin Berthe's husband], who had already been living in Illinois, assured her that soon she'd forget all her troubles. In a brave attempt to conquer her fears, she looked up and around again and thought, "This does, after all, look just like the sky in Stavanger."

Synva was the next of the Thue children to be summoned to North Dakota. In 1903, several months after her brother Perry had gone to Illinois, twenty-year-old Synva embarked alone, departing from Bergen by way of England to Ellis Island. She then spent several more days on a train from New York to North Dakota. Unlike Martha and Perry, who had made the journey to join cousins and countrymen in Waukegan, Synva was compelled by her father to work on the farm near Uncle Helge's home in Horace to earn back the cost of her transatlantic passage. Upon her arrival, her uncle and aunt stripped her, sprayed her down, and burned all her clothes for fear of contagion—a welcome that would distress and offend her for the rest of her life.

Synva had more ambitious intentions than being a farm worker, and if she were to persuade Uncle Helge to allow her to pursue a nursing education in nearby Fargo, she needed someone to replace her on the farm. She summoned Martha from Illinois, but Martha turned out to hate farm work as much as Synva did. She asked her father to send sixteen-year-old Astrid to replace her. Thus, in 1904, Astrid made the trip to North Dakota.

---

5. The Norwegian word *moster* means "mother's sister" or "maternal aunt."

The three sisters would work at the nearby farm until they had gotten on their feet. Those years were etched in their minds as some of the hardest of their lives, salvaged only by the family camaraderie among the backbreaking work. But, thanks to the early efforts of the three elder sisters, the younger Thue girls wouldn't have to work on a farm to stake their own claims in America.

By 1908, all three of the sisters had married men they'd met right there in Cass County: Synva wed a Norwegian named Martin J. Quam, Martha a Norwegian named Nils Brakke, and Astrid a Swede, John Rydgren. Having found their mates, the sisters went their separate ways.

Astrid and John moved to Fargo, where they raised three children, Agnes, Elsie, and John. Martha and Nils settled in a town called McVille, North Dakota, which at the time contained nothing but a railroad. They raised four children, Liv, Adelaide, Nils, and Perry. Upon finishing her nursing studies in Fargo, Synva went with Martin to a relatively new settlement called Walker, Minnesota, where they spent the rest of their lives. Martin eventually owned a general store and a good deal of real estate, and Synva worked as a registered nurse, first for the town doctor and later for Ah-Gwah-Ching, a tuberculosis sanatorium. Their adopted daughter, Margaret, died of rheumatic fever at age thirteen. Synva and Martin also cared for Lily Maurstad as a daughter, when Synva's cousin John Maurstad left Minnesota for Alaska. Later, John returned to take Lily to Alaska and Synva grieved her absence. As the eldest daughter, Synva was very much the maternal figure of the Thue clan, and she always longed to have children in her home.

In the village of Åheim, with her five eldest siblings already gone to America, Gudrun was just beginning her life. Her first home was high up on a mountain plateau, overlooking a sparkling lake that froze in the winter to allow safe passage clear to the other side. Skiing and ice-skating were the most common means of fun and transportation.

When Gudrun was only three, her family moved about 180 kilometers north of Åheim to the maritime center of Molde. They settled on a farm in the town of Hjelset, where some of the family's descendants live to this day. Molde was a growing tourist and trade destination and the site of one of the country's first hydroelectric power plants, established in 1909. Gudrun would later tell her children about her amazement at lighting a whole room at the flick of a switch. She and her siblings basked in Molde's unseasonably high winter temperatures, where the snow would melt when it hit the ground. The city's topography—mountains to the east and west and hills to the north—shelters the city with its 220 snow-clad peaks, creating a temperate climate and an abundance of lush vegetation unusual for such a northern latitude.

Gudrun and her close siblings—Ingeborg, Ragnhild, Bård, and Borghild—shared an idyllic childhood on Norway's west coast. She and her sisters and brother fished for salmon, coalfish, cod, haddock, mackerel, trout, and more in the lakes, rivers, and fjords. Wandering along the gentle mountain terrain, through meadows full of berries, they kept an eye out for mischievous trolls. Along Nordfjord's beaches they trekked in the footsteps of Vikings in summer and ice-skated over their watery graves in the winter. In the dark winter months the children would read and do needlepoint and *hardangersøm* embroidery by candlelight, while summertime in the Land of the Midnight Sun was full of days that never ended. Even now much of this area on Nordfjord remains largely unspoiled.

As a little girl Gudrun loved to sing and had an angelic voice. One day when she was swimming in the fjord by her house, she nearly drowned. Frantic, her family dragged her out of the water. Numerous tries at resuscitating her seemed to fail, but her mother insisted they continue until, finally, she coughed up water and came to. Gudrun always recalled hearing her mother's voice telling them, "Don't give up!" For some reason, after this incident she could no longer sing. Instead she whistled like a bird, and a day never went by without her whistling a tune. As an adult she would whistle like a construction worker, loudly enough to call her children to come home to eat from blocks away.

Borghild, Bård, and Gudrun in Molde

As a child and the baby of the family, Gudrun was always very close to her parents. To a teacher's daughter, education was of prime importance, a value she would instill in her children and that they too would pass on. She was especially intent on learning the magic her mother made in the kitchen. For her, kitchen duty was never a chore, but a pleasure.

In Minnesota, Synva was unable to have children and was lonely for her family, so she asked her mother to send her little sister Borghild to live with her in America. Their mother believed Borghild, only nine years old at the time, was too young to leave home. But Ragnhild was sixteen and eager to grow up, so she volunteered to join her sister across the Atlantic in Borghild's place. Thus, in 1909 Ragnhild took the long journey to Walker, Minnesota, by way of Quebec.

Around the same time, a distinguished hotelier named Kristoffer Stensrud courted and won Gudrun's sister Ingeborg; he married her and took her to Oslo. The couple later ran one of Europe's most famous and historic hotels, the Hotel Britannia in Trondheim, which hosts foreign dignitaries and royalty to this day.

Leangen gård ved Trondhjem.

20/15
Eneret Mittet &

A postcard of Leangen Gård where Ingeborg and Kristoffer lived. Located right beside the fjord, it was occupied by the German army during World War II.

And so, before Gudrun reached ten years of age, the number of siblings still in Norway had shrunk to three. Bård, Borghild, and Gudrun finished their schooling and followed their own pursuits. Bård and several subsequent generations stayed on the family farm in Hjelset. Borghild went to Botne, Vestfold, near Oslo, and became a nurse for the Norwegian Red Cross. While still in her teens, Gudrun went to live with Ingeborg and Kristoffer in Oslo and experienced big-city living for the first time.

At the same time the last Thue children were crossing into adulthood, European imperial powers had reached a boiling point, thrusting the world community into World War I. As the United States initially did, Norway declared its neutrality, but during the Battle of the Atlantic from 1914 to 1918, the seas around Norway ran amok with submarine warfare and mining; the North Sea was blockaded and the Norwegian merchant fleet sustained heavy losses. The Great War brought deep economic hardship to Norway and much of the rest of the world,

Gudrun Thue around the time of her confirmation in Molde

and the hard times continued into the early 1920s. Although spread across the Atlantic Ocean, Gudrun's big, tight-knit family endured as families do. They stuck together.

Gudrun longed to know her family in America, some of whom she had never met. Letters and visits from siblings and cousins were a mainstay in her life. Enter Jofrid Maurstad, a spirited cousin who would set the course of three Thue sisters' lives in many ways. Jofrid's main residence was Brooklyn, New York, where she would later work as a cook for Grace Kelly and Prince Rainier. She had a habit of popping by to visit her cousins in America and convincing them to go with her to the next destination. Around 1916, she stopped in to see Synva and Ragnhild in Walker, Minnesota, and took Ragnhild with her to visit Martha in North Dakota. Ragnhild stayed in North Dakota for seven years, until 1922 when Jofrid once again dropped in. This time she took Ragnhild back to Norway for a fateful visit.

This was Ragnhild's only trip back home since she'd left thirteen years earlier. She was now almost thirty years old and had come a long way from the eager-to-grow-up teenage girl her mother remembered. Reunited, the family had a wonderful time, and Ragnhild stayed for many months, bonding with her sisters as if she had never left. But soon America was calling her back. In the midst of Europe's continent-wide depression resulting from World War I, work was hard to come by. Norwegian wages paled in comparison to what was achievable in the United States. Later, Ragnhild would explain her return simply: "I had to get a job!" But this time she wouldn't make the trip alone.

With some enticement from Jofrid and Ragnhild, Borghild and Gudrun decided they wanted to see what all the fuss was about. They hoped to make some money, have some adventures, and come back to Norway after two or three years. Gudrun especially wanted to meet the sisters she'd known only through letters and packages. Gudrun's mother, who was sixty-five years old then, saw them off with the same heartache she'd felt upon the departure of so many of her other children. Gudrun promised her mother she would be back.

And so their new adventures began. The three young women left from Oslo in 1923 and took the ten-day trip across the ocean on a ship filled with young, educated, single Scandinavians like themselves, some of whom they would meet again stateside. They disembarked at Ellis Island and decided to stay in Brooklyn for a while.[6]

The Thue sisters had stepped out of depressed, war-torn Europe and into America's Roaring Twenties. Everything seemed possible. The decade following the end of the horrific First World War had ushered in political and economic reforms, including Prohibition, woman suffrage, and laissez-faire economic policies. It was "mass" everything: mass production, mass broadcasting media (radio and film), mass marketing, mass electrification, mass urbanization, and mass transit. Expressways lined with telephone wires now connected the masses to affordable goods and services, and to each other. And nowhere did the twenties roar more loudly than in New York City.

Within this giant metropolis were close-knit neighborhoods where ethnicities congregated, as if the city were a microcosm of the world and each neighborhood a country with its own language, culture, and customs. "Little Norway," as the area originally settled by Norwegian seamen was known until the 1970s, was situated in Brooklyn's Sunset Park neighborhood along Eighth Avenue from 45th to 60th Streets. Little Norway's main street, lined with Norwegian bakeries and specialty stores and host to enthusiastic parades on Leif Erikson Day and Norwegian Independence Day, was affectionately called Lapskaus Boulevard, named after a Norwegian beef stew. Norwegian organizations, churches, and social service institutions flourished. The residents had imported their own version of a Norwegian parish, where they helped one another, lived, worshiped, ate, and made merry together, and from which they contributed to the greater American community they now called home. For example, the world-famous New York subway system was designed by the Norwegian immigrant Sverre Dahm; the twelve-story double-spiral staircase in the Statue of Liberty was designed and installed by the Norwegian American Carl Michael Eger's firm Hecla; and Ole Singstad was the chief engineer in the design of the Holland Tunnel, the Lincoln Tunnel, the Queens Midtown Tunnel, and the Brooklyn Battery Tunnel.

---

6. Gudrun's daughter, Irene, always thought Gudrun had arrived in 1919. Ellis Island and Bergen passenger lists report that the trip was made in 1923.

Gudrun and her sisters were the new girls in town, and even after a lifetime in America, they would keep Norwegian accents as thick as the day they stepped off the boat. By now Gudrun was a proper Scandinavian beauty, five foot five with blond hair and soft blue eyes. She and her pair of petite, lively brunette sisters stayed in the Norway House, a boarding house in Little Norway for newly arriving countrymen. Friendly and sweet, Gudrun loved a good laugh with an extra dose of silliness. Her sister Ragnhild was sharp-tongued, witty, and strong-minded. Borghild played the accordion, sang, and composed music. She often got lost in constant musings, but she was also astute enough to frustrate her sisters by snatching their latest flapper fashions before they got a chance to wear them.

The Thue women soon found work as domestic help and were having a ball in Brooklyn, enjoying a good livelihood and a brimming social life. Decades later, in 1963, Gudrun's daughter, Irene, planned a trip to New York, to show her mom the big city and buy her some fashionable suits before a transatlantic cruise to Norway. She'd forgotten her mother was no stranger to New York City. Irene was put in her place when Gudrun dragged her all over the city and never once consulted the subway map. Gudrun could never forget New York City. It was the birthplace of her own American dream.

But working for wealthy New Yorkers had its drawbacks. As Ragnhild recalled, Gudrun was the only one of them who could keep a job. She was the conscientious one, meticulous about everything she did. Ragnhild, on the other hand, would quickly lose patience when the lady of the house would trail behind her as she worked, pointing out the spots she missed. Her jobs didn't last long before she would pocket her five-buck salary and never go back.

Borghild, a Red Cross nurse by profession and a free spirit by nature, was no better suited to the job. Lost in her daydreams one afternoon, she knocked over a priceless lamp in her wealthy employer's home. Rather than face the lady and gentleman of the house, Borghild ran home to persuade her sisters that now was the perfect time to try out a new city—*right now!*

Gudrun and Ragnhild wanted to stay. They were at the center of the universe! But Borghild, desperate to avoid an eternity cleaning houses to pay for a lamp, made a good sales pitch: Chicago was full of Norwegians, at the time with the largest Norwegian population in the world after Oslo and Bergen, and they had lots of family there. There were plenty of good jobs in Chicago and a healthy supply of eligible Norwegian bachelors. What more could they ask for? And so the Thue girls headed west.

Chicago's Little Norway had grown on the northwest side, in the Humboldt Park and Logan Square area, and was a major cultural and organizational center of America's Norwegian community. The Chicago newspaper *Skandinaven*, founded in 1866, would become the largest Norwegian-language journal in the world. Chicago's Norwegians increasingly comprised professional men and women, including health professionals, journalists, engineers, architects, and others with technical and artistic skills. The Norge Ski Club formed in Humboldt Park, and the main social hub was the elegant Norwegian-American Club.

Upon their arrival the Thue women stayed with their cousin Berthe Faleide, who also helped them find jobs. Fortunately for everyone, Borghild found work as a nurse at the Norwegian American Hospital. Ragnhild worked at a general store, and Gudrun worked in River Forest as a governess and energetic housekeeper for the wealthy Dwight Austin family (Austin was an executive with the Great Atlantic & Pacific Tea Company, later A&P). After a short time with that family, Gudrun moved on to another job as a governess in a well-to-do Chicago neighborhood. She remained there for many years, becoming part of the family. Even after she had her own family, she displayed a picture of those children in her home.

Like New York, Chicago was highly segregated by nationality, race, and ethnicity, but revelers of all kinds mingled behind locked doors, around dark corners, and in shadowy tunnels under North Avenue where the cash and booze flowed freely. Above ground, the Thue girls danced their evenings away at the Norwegian-American Club, where gangsters didn't exist. So, when Gudrun heard people on the train talking about speakeasies, she thought, "Perfect. I don't speak English very well." When she asked her cab driver where to find one, he became indignant and demanded she remove herself from his cab.

This photo was taken at the Norwegian-American Club in Chicago in the early 1930s. Gudrun is in the middle, and Borghild is across from her.

Young suitors would take the girls out to stroll down North Avenue, stopping for a bite or to listen to jazz tunes. Eventually, two suitors stood out from the others. Peder Hoye, a Norwegian engineer, swept Ragnhild off her feet. Then Ragnhild came home one day to find Borghild on the front steps, too busy smooching a young man to bother to say hello. That was how she met Borghild's future husband, Amund Fjortoft. Fjortoft, as they called him, was a graduate of architecture school in Trondheim, worked as an architect for the city of Chicago, and was a talented artist. Ragnhild and Peder married and had two children, Sylvia and Burton; Borghild and Amund married and had three children, Inge, Edmund John, and Ruth Emily. They would call Chicago home for the rest of their lives.

Just as the Thue sisters were beginning to chart their futures, the glorious 1920s crashed, leaving the wreckage of the Great Depression. Luckily, Gudrun's wealthy employers escaped the destitution that befell the working class of Chicago, and as their governess she enjoyed job security that many others did not. One day the family's cook fell ill, and Gudrun was asked to cook in her place. She served up a magnificent roast pork chop dinner, and the family raved about her dish, immediately hiring her as their chef. In the years that followed, the kitchen became her studio, where she perfected her art and taught herself to express creativity, personality, and care in each dish. When the family traveled, they would offer Gudrun their lavish mansion to enjoy, and Gudrun would fill the formal dining table with her sisters and their husbands, her cousins, and friends. They would feast on roast turkey with all the trimmings and then dream between silk sheets. Pretending to be filthy rich for the weekend provided a stark contrast to the squalor that engulfed the city outside the mansion gates.

Gudrun's father sent her this letter from Norway in December 1932. Irene found the letter by accident years later between the pages of one of Gudrun's cookbooks.

Gudrun's promise to her mother to return home weighed on her often, and she had returned once, in 1928, to see her. Norway was her motherland, but America was her future. In 1934, she was devastated to learn that her mother had passed away at age seventy-five. She and Synva traveled to Molde to grieve with their father and the rest of their family. (Fourteen years later, in September 1948, Bottolf Thue died. Daughter Martha was at his side, having made the trip by plane from America, as were daughter Ingeborg and son Bård.)

Though Gudrun would always feel pangs of longing and regret for not having kept her promise to return to Norway, she knew her mother had understood the cycle of life: children grow up, move on, and build their own lives, sometimes in far-off places, but a family always remains together in spirit. Gudrun chose to immortalize her mother in the traditions she taught her children, cultivated in the kitchen, shared around the dining table, and carried on for generations to come.

It is said that when one suffers a devastating loss, the heart makes way for an even deeper love. For Gudrun, this love came in the form of the dapper Øyvind (called Irving) Sandvold, a few years younger than she. (By now Gudrun was approaching her mid-thirties, and her sisters teased her that she'd be an old maid unless she stopped being so picky.) Six feet four, with a distinguished brow and thick brown hair, Irving was the son of a furniture maker. He not only could build and repair anything but was also a champion ski jumper and a flautist in a Norwegian orchestra.

The two met thanks to Borghild, who worked with Irving's sister, Aslaug, at the Norwegian American Hospital. After a bit of behind-the-scenes matchmaking, their romance began with an introduction at the Norwegian-American Club. They made each other laugh and shared values and interests: together, they were complete. Without further ado, Gudrun and Irving went to the Lutheran minister's house and were married beneath the apple tree in his yard in July 1936. And with that, every last Thue sister had found her mate.

The newlyweds settled in Irving Park, Chicago. Irving was in business with his brother Sverre, known as Sandy, picking up chickens and eggs from farms in Wisconsin, sorting, candling, and packaging them, and delivering them to distributors in Chicago for consumption: a vital service in a Depression-proof food industry. He and his brother had arrived at Ellis Island in 1929 with not much more than fifty cents between them. Like Gudrun's sisters, Irving had worked off his passage on a farm in Wisconsin, saved up some money, and moved to Chicago.

Gudrun resigned from her position with the wealthy Chicago family to become a housewife, and, soon, a mother. On December 10, 1937, Irene Olivia Adelaide Sandvold was born. Gudrun wanted to call her daughter Ingeborg, after her mother and sister, but Aslaug, probably speaking from experience, insisted that Americans would never be able to pronounce it. Sandy suggested Irene, after the actress Irene Dunne, and Gudrun agreed. (Ironically, Irene always wished her name was Ingeborg and years later gave that name to her daughter.) A year and a half later, on May 17, 1939, Syttende Mai, Edward Oliver Thue Sandvold was born, named for Irving's father, Edvard. The young family spent its early years in a tightly knit Chicago community, surrounded by friends and relatives, building a loving and comfortable home in the midst of the Great Depression.

And then, with the bombing of Pearl Harbor, Japan drew the United States into the global conflict that had been devastating Europe and Asia for years. For the Sandvolds, this was deeply personal. On a train trip with Synva and their father after her mother's funeral, Gudrun had passed through Germany and glimpsed the country's metamorphosis into a military industrial complex; from her window on the train she had seen soldiers training and marching in formation, a procession of tanks and artillery. By 1941 Gudrun and Irving's parents and siblings back in Norway had been suffering for nearly two years under German occupation.

Leangen Gård, an estate and farm in Trondheim owned by Gudrun's sister Ingeborg, was commandeered by Nazi soldiers for the duration of the war. Ingeborg's sons, Thore, Nils, and Per Stensrud, along with many others in the Thue family and across Norway, volunteered in the Norwegian underground, risking their lives to resist the occupation. Led by their Norwegian government-in-exile in London, the resistance forces launched military defenses and counterattacks, commando raids, and sabotage missions, at times carried out by soldiers who would disappear into the snowy night on skis. Among these acts of sabotage were the destruction of Norsk Hydro's Vemork power plant, which produced heavy water, and the sinking of the ferry *Hydro* as it moved a shipment of heavy water to Germany—both of which disrupted German plans to build an atomic bomb. Norwegians also resisted in the form of civil disobedience and unarmed resistance, through counterpropaganda publications and radio broadcasts. All of these activities came at great personal risk, as the Germans retaliated by executing and imprisoning innocent Norwegians who resisted them.

Edward Oliver Sandvold (age two) and Irene Olivia Adelaide Sandvold (age three and a half). This photograph may have been taken by a family member in Irving Park, Illinois, before their move to Wisconsin.

Ingeborg's son Thore served as a pilot in the Norwegian Naval Air Force. He trained in Little Norway in Canada and flew missions along the Norwegian Coast from airfields in England and Scotland. Her son Nils, a medical student at the University of Oslo, was arrested along with most other male students there in November 1943, following an act of arson on campus by a resistance group. He narrowly escaped being sent to Germany and instead spent until July 1944 in two prison camps close to Oslo.

A Sandvold family portrait taken in Fort Atkinson sometime during Word War II. Front row: Eddie, Gudrun, Irene. Back row: Irving, Thore Stensrud (Ingeborg's son)

Meanwhile, Ingeborg's son Per remained in Trondheim; he was arrested and sent to a prison camp on three occasions and was interrogated by Nazi occupiers, who tortured him with starvation, beatings, and bindings that cut off his circulation. He survived, but he suffered from poor health for the rest of his life.

A couple of years into the war, Irving, who had been a soldier in the Norwegian Army, was called up for the U.S. Army draft. Irene and Eddie were still very little, and by now the Sandvold family had left Chicago for the small Wisconsin town of Fort Atkinson. With fear and trepidation, Gudrun and the children prepared themselves for his departure. But the army decided that Irving's egg business was providing vital and necessary commodities and that he should stay home. The same business that had shielded his family to some degree from the devastating effects of the Great Depression also served to keep the family together in a time of great global peril.

After nearly twenty years in big cities, Gudrun considered Fort Atkinson a bit of a homecoming: a return to the farm life of her youth, albeit without the fjords and sprawling mountains. After several years in town, the family purchased a seven-acre farm with a hatchery on Riverside Drive, where Irving expanded his business into chicken and egg production. He continued to pick up chickens and eggs from farmers throughout Wisconsin and bring them to his hatchery along with the chickens and eggs he now produced. There his employees sorted, candled, processed, and packaged them. Irving would often accept barters as payment from customers who couldn't pay, a practice that allowed the Sandvolds to build a menagerie of farm animals including two ponies, named Duke and Duchess, and a family of white Peking ducks. Their miniature zoo also included a beloved Chesapeake dog named Queenie and a brood of chickens, chicks, and geese. The family also raised chickens and eggs for their own consumption. Nearly every day Gudrun would kill and pluck a chicken to serve for dinner the same night. Preservatives were completely foreign to them.

Irving's brother Sverre (called Sandy) lived nearby, and Gudrun was friends with Sandy's wife, Lucille, and Lucille's mother. Irene and Eddie grew up with Sandy's son Dale Erik, who was a bit younger than they, and with whom they shared a school, church, and many of the same friends. Dale Erik had a great fondness for *Tante* (Aunt) Gudrun. One of his earliest memories of her was when he was five years old. His parents had had a baby girl who died after only twelve hours. That night, Gudrun took him outside under the starry night sky. "Look up at that bright light," she said to Dale Erik, pointing at the brightest star. "That's your little sister."

Eddie and Irene grew up gathering around the radio in the family room, until Irving brought home the family's first TV when the kids were teenagers. Music was central to the family, with Irene and Eddie playing piano, Irving playing flute and accordion, and Eddie singing. Sometimes, just to shake things up, Gudrun would switch the furniture from the dining room to the family room and vice versa. The formal living room was used only for guests and during Christmastime to dance around the massive live Christmas tree that barely fit through the front door and, when erected, would mash up against the ceiling.

The big yard made a perfect badminton court in the summer and snowball battlefield in the winter, and their artesian well, whose water remained just above 32 degrees all year round, held a collection of incessantly croaking frogs. The kids fished and boated on the river across the street almost every day and ran across the big field behind the house to kick rocks and catch frogs in the creek. They swam, played sports, picked apples, cared for their animals, and climbed trees. There was never a shortage of things to do until they heard their mother's unmistakable whistle. "*Vær så god:* Dinner's ready!"

Gudrun filled the Sandvold home with the aromas of almond-rich desserts, oven-baked bread, and freshly brewed coffee. The basement was home to all of Gudrun's fresh canned goods, jams and jellies, watermelon pickles, cucumber pickles, pickled peaches—pickled everything!—and her dining table was always set, at its center a cut-glass crystal bowl filled with fresh lilies of the valley. But it was Gudrun's spacious kitchen, which housed both a new electric stove and an old-fashioned wood-burning stove, that was the center of the home. This was where friends and family would congregate around a big kitchen table over coffee and open-faced sandwiches.

Irving worked close enough to home to pop in throughout the day and refuel with a cup of coffee and a kiss on the cheek. It wasn't unusual for friends and neighbors, members of the church, parents of schoolmates, and employees and business associates to stop by for a snack, and at dinner Gudrun always set an extra plate just in case. She always cooked too much food and insisted on second and third helpings, filling her guests' plates even as they said no. Sandy was the only one who could stop her, and only by placing his hand on his plate and keeping it there.

Gudrun's reputation as a cook preceded her. At school picnics she would deliver roasters full of chicken, enough to feed the entire teaching staff—twice. As Dale Erik said, "No one could do chicken like Gudrun. They've tried, but they could never duplicate it." She cooked for the ladies of her church, for big special occasions, for birthdays and holidays, and sometimes just for fun.

Gudrun regarded nourishing her children, body and soul, as her most important and fulfilling task. Irene grew into an accomplished student and musician. Eddie grew as tall as his father and became one of the top athletes in Wisconsin, earning a full basketball scholarship to the University of Wisconsin. He was also class valedictorian and a talented singer, musician, and actor. Gudrun diligently documented every one of their successes in her scrapbooks, taking immense pride and satisfaction in the people they were growing up to be.

The Sandvold and Fjortoft families in front of *Tante* Synva's house in Walker, Minnesota, 1954. From left: Ruth Emily Fjortoft (Saksvig), Irving Sandvold, Gudrun Thue Sandvold, Amund Fjortoft, Borghild Thue Fjortoft, Eddie Sandvold, Synva Thue Quam, Irene Sandvold.

Irving's sister Aslaug (*Tante* Asse) and her husband, George Moe, would drive up from Chicago every Thursday in good weather, and Borghild and her family visited at least once a month. Borghild's daughter Ruthie was just one month and ten days older than Irene, and whenever it was time for the Fjortofts to head home, the children would hide Ruthie so they wouldn't be able to leave. Once, they boated so far down the river, it was hours before the adults could track them down. They always got into trouble for their antics, but that never stopped them from trying to keep Ruthie as long as they could. Ruthie and Irene were so dear to each other that when they grew up they named their daughters after each other. Gudrun and Borghild's lifelong bond has carried from generation to generation.

The Sandvolds regularly visited family in Chicago and Minnesota. On one occasion, Gudrun had made Ragnhild's favorite birthday cake and carried it on her lap the whole way from Fort Atkinson to Chicago, cringing with every bump in the road, until finally they pulled up to Ragnhild's house—where Irving promptly dropped the cake upside down on the sidewalk. Poor Irving never lived it down.

Gudrun's care packages followed Irene and Eddie to the University of Wisconsin, where Irene took after her *Tantes* Synva, Borghild, and Asse and pursued nursing. Eddie, meanwhile, was interested in everything. He went from chemical engineering to business, transferred to pre-med and zoology to qualify for medical school, and finally majored in zoology.

But Eddie had no problem deciding on his wife-to-be. Petite, brunette Karen had been Eddie's classmate since kindergarten, and Gudrun had subliminally encouraged this romance the entire time. By the time they fell in love in their sophomore year of college, they already knew everything about each other, their families knew each other, and they had nearly twenty years of friendship as a foundation.

Irene had inherited the adventurous spirit that carried Gudrun from a small farm in western Norway across the ocean and from one big city to the next, and after working as a nurse in Madison for a year or so, she decided to go to San Francisco. It was the sixties, and as Chicago and New York had been forty years earlier, San Francisco was the center of the universe.

With her mother and *Tante* Borghild, Irene planned to zigzag through the south to see every relative and friend they could between Wisconsin and California. Dale Erik, in college in Kansas at the time, expected them every day for almost a week, but still they hadn't arrived. When they finally showed up, Irene explained that they'd seen a pretty little road and decided to see where it would go. The trip to San Francisco took a full three weeks.

The Sandvold family at Grauman's Chinese restaurant in Los Angeles, during the drive to San Francisco when Irene moved to California in 1961. Clockwise around the table from left front: Little Gudrun Thue Hickey, Irene, Gudrun, Borghild Thue Fjortoft, Little Borghild Thue Wyzga, Wes Wyzga, Melissa (Little Gudrun's granddaughter), and John Hickey (Little Gudrun's husband).

Irene didn't stop traveling once she reached San Francisco. She journeyed to New Mexico, Washington, D.C., Baltimore, and South Vietnam, then to Belfast, Northern Ireland, and back to Washington, D.C., and Baltimore, where she would earn a doctorate in public health. Irene married a handsome, worldly Norwegian-American Foreign Service officer named Lars Hydle, with whom she had two children, Lars Sandvold Hydle and Ingeborg Louise Ruth Hydle. Her new husband not only appreciated Irene's Nordic beauty, her cooking, and her intelligence, but he loved her lack of pretension, noting, "In any relationship, I had enough pretension and vanity for two."

Eddie and Karen worked in Madison for several years before moving to Boulder, Colorado. There they raised two boys, Erik and Quinn. When the boys were still little, Gudrun and Irving moved to Boulder and became managers of the apartment complex where Eddie and Karen lived before buying a house. Irving maintained the complex and worked part-time at McGuckin Hardware Store, while Gudrun doled out goodies and conversation to the various tenants in the building. They soon knew everyone in the complex by their first names.

Gudrun had grown up in an era when the lady of the house always wore house-dresses, so each day she curled her hair and put on red lipstick and a dress. However, by the sixties and seventies, women were wearing pants and pantsuits. Karen suggested that Gudrun try wearing pants, since they were comfortable and they would keep her legs warm. Gudrun would say, "Noooo, I can't do that! No way! I'll never wear them, you can be sure of that!" But in her own way, Gudrun quietly joined the women's liberation movement: one day she answered the door sporting a handsome pair of slacks.

Gudrun and Irving played a big part in their grandchildren's lives. Erik and Quinn, who called their grandparents Gigi and Boppa, slept over at their house at least once a month, and nearly every Sunday they would eat and spend time together. Irving built a cigar stand with a secret compartment, where the boys found a new treat every time they came over. As much as Gudrun loved to indulge the boys, she loved to teach them as well. If a public announcement or a presidential address would come on the television, she would tell them, "You must watch it, boys! It's history!" When Irene's son Lars was a toddler, Irene came home from work to find a fresh Hullabaloo (Gudrun's term for snack time) on the table and Gudrun going down the stairs, backward, on her hands and knees, teaching the baby how to scale the staircase without falling.

In 1971, Gudrun and Irving, Eddie's family, and Irene, who was still single at the time, traveled to Norway together. After almost forty years of marriage, this was the first time Gudrun and Irving had seen each other's hometowns and met each other's families in Norway. They had grown up in towns five hours apart, yet only connected twenty years and thousands of miles later. It was a memorable trip. In Irving's hometown of Gjøvik, Erik caught his first fish in Lake Mjøsa, a perch, which Gudrun cooked right up. One day, Eddie drove the family along the mountains in Trollstigveien in a thick, treacherous fog. Gudrun was petrified. "Oh, mama mia," she said, gripping Eddie with all her might. "Mama mia! Oh, Eddie! I'm so scared! Eddie, I'm terrified! I can't see a thing!" Eddie replied, "Don't worry, Mom. I can't either," and she laughed so hard she wasn't scared anymore.

Over the years, Gudrun and Irving became deeply interdependent. She made a grocery list, he went to the store and picked out the freshest and best ingredients he could find, and she would make whatever dish he craved. She never learned to drive, but she loved getting out of the house. With a little nudging, Irving would take her wherever she wanted to go, especially on Sunday drives up in the mountains. But they rarely ate out: the best meals Irving could have were made by Gudrun in his own kitchen.

Gudrun lived through technological advances from automobiles and airplanes to electricity and telephones to radio and television. She'd lived on two continents, traveling from the fjords of Norway to the world's biggest cities to the farms and mountains of the American West. She saw the roles of women evolve from the basic right to vote to economic, social, and political participation—from housedresses to trousers. She endured two world wars, a decades-long cold war, a great depression, and a cultural revolution. Through it all, she cultivated a loving, devoted marriage and successfully raised two children, while taking every opportunity to connect with her fellow man through caring conversation, a good laugh, and a plate of chocolate chip cookies. Gudrun's was a fruitful life, full of love, family, and friendship, simple pleasures, and great food. And when Gudrun, Irene, and Eddie were in the kitchen together, it was hard to tell where Gudrun's cooking ended and her children's cooking began.

Gudrun's greatest joy was welcoming people into her life with food and friendship. Her recipes embody the love that she put into everything she did.

# PART II
## Recipes and Traditions

NORWEGIAN TABLE PRAYER

| | |
|---|---|
| *I Jesu navn går vi til bords* | In Jesus' name to the table we go |
| *å spise, drikke på ditt ord.* | To eat and drink according to His word. |
| *Deg Gud til ære, oss til gavn,* | To God the honor, us the gain, |
| *Så får vi mat i Jesu navn.* | So we have food in Jesus' name. |
| *Amen.* | Amen. |

In the dining room on Riverside Drive. From left front: Irving, Eddie (age seven), Irene (age eight), Gudrun (caught at one of the rare times that she was seated during a meal), unknown, and Paul Junghans

# *Familie Selskap* (Family Get-Togethers)

## Special Occasions
- 🏵 **Christmas**
- 🏵 **Weddings**

## Everyday Meals and Snacks
- 🏵 *Frokost:* **The Breakfast of (Ski) Champions**
  - Gudrun's Crepes Suzette
  - Gudrun's French Toast
  - Gudrun's Pancakes
  - Norwegian Coffee Waffles

- 🏵 **The Hullabaloo**
  - Homemade Hot Chocolate
  - Spiced Nuts

- 🏵 *Nattmat*

- 🏵 *Smørbrød*
  - Gjetost
  - Homemade Mayonnaise I
  - Homemade Mayonnaise II
  - Tomato and Cheese *Smørbrød*
  - Tomato and Egg *Smørbrød*
  - Butter and Chive *Smørbrød*
  - Carrot and Pea *Smørbrød*
  - Celery and Radish *Smørbrød*
  - Cream Cheese and Vegetable *Smørbrød*
  - Smoked Salmon and Scrambled Egg *Smørbrød*

Pickled Herring and Egg *Smørbrød*

Sardine or Mackerel and Egg *Smørbrød*

Salad Shrimp *Smørbrød*

Anchovy and Egg *Smørbrød*

Shrimp and Mayonnaise *Smørbrød*

Pickled Herring *Smørbrød*

Smoked Herring and Egg *Smørbrød*

Salami and Cucumber *Smørbrød*

*Pariser* (*Smørbrød* with Seasoned Ground Beef)

# SPECIAL OCCASIONS

Smörgåsbord is perhaps the best-known Scandinavian word in America, thanks in no small part to the Swedish Chef of Muppets notoriety. The word has even become a part of the lexicon to describe any variety of choices from which one can pick and choose. This is, in fact, just what it is—an all-you-can-eat buffet full of more varieties of food than anyone could ever eat by herself! The *smörgåsbord*, a staple of all special occasions, lets guests know that the cook has gone all out and is eager to please whatever the craving of the day may be. Any large get-together is an occasion for a *smörgåsbord*, and the fundamental concept is inclusiveness: cold foods, hot foods, appetizers, salads, jellies, cheeses, assorted pickled goods, smoked seafood, meats and game, desserts, ad infinitum. A *smörgåsbord* of the Gudrun variety includes four or five dishes out of each food category, always to include *smørbrød* (open-faced sandwiches), Norwegian meatballs, *fiskeboller* (fish balls), herring and salmon, fruit soup, *rømmegrøt* (sour cream porridge), and a broad array of desserts.

We usually were so satisfied from our meal, and the salads and vegetables that went with it, that we did not crave dessert. That came later, or with coffee at varied times during the day—but not with our main meal.

We always ate together around the kitchen table. Our mother would keep serving to be sure we had everything piping hot, and we could not get her to sit down until we were nearing the end of the meal. As soon as our plates were clean she would come with seconds (or thirds), and if we said we couldn't eat anymore, she would say with a sad face, "Oh, you didn't like it."

## CHRISTMAS

Christmas is a month-long cooking bonanza that begins right after Thanksgiving, when zillions of *krumkaker*, or crisp Norwegian waffle cookies, are made and distributed to friends and relatives both near and far. In Gudrun's house, a dinner on Christmas Eve, or *julaften*, would inevitably start with the *koldtbord* (cold board) delicacies of *smørbrød*, assorted cheeses and flat bread (our family liked the Ideal brand), and salmon and herring. The Christmas fish, *lutefisk*, is served swimming in melted butter and often accompanied by boiled potatoes and sliced cucumber salad. Christmas morning breakfast centers around the pastry called a *kringle* (a coffee cake with many thin layers of buttery pastry, filled with almond paste or jam), plus coffee and milk, soft- and hard-cooked eggs in egg cups, grapefruit halves topped with a maraschino cherry, and other breakfast assortments. Christmas Day, or *juledag,* dinner begins with a fruit soup and *smørbrød* and includes hearty fish, game, and meat dishes, creamed potatoes, and other vegetables. After dinner, coffee accompanies an overload of flavored cookies, macaroons and tarts, cream cakes, *julekake* (Norwegian Christmas bread), *berlinerkranser* (Norwegian butter knot cookies), *fattigmannsbakkels* (fried, spiced Norwegian cookies), *sandbakkels* (crisp butter cookies baked in a special tin), and marzipan pigs and fruit candies. For Gudrun, Christmas was complete only when family and friends joined hands and danced around the Christmas tree.

## WEDDINGS

Generous as the menus are for *smörgåsbords* and Christmas, there is no better occasion than a wedding to go completely overboard. For Gudrun, this meant staggering amounts of *krumkaker, kransekaker,* and Norwegian meatballs. When Eddie and Karen announced their intention to have their wedding on December 17, she was dumbfounded. She had just gotten over the fact that her son was getting married while still in college, but now a Christmas wedding? After all, Christmas by itself was a monthlong event, a daily cooking extravaganza ending only after New Year's Day. To manage both a proper Christmas and a proper wedding was going to take a miracle. Gudrun made several *kransekaker,* to double as a table decoration and a delicious dessert, and for the wedding reception she cooked more than five hundred *krumkaker,* which she kept in people's freezers all over Fort Atkinson.

She again commandeered the community's kitchens when Irene was married. By this time, she and Irving were apartment managers, and she stored hundreds of Norwegian meatballs in freezers all over the apartment complex. But when the wedding day came and Gudrun went around to collect the wedding meatballs, one of the tenants had eaten them all! The hungry tenant must have thought it was one of the goodies Gudrun was known to dole out for no particular reason. (Of course, Gudrun immediately began to make hundreds more meatballs.)

# EVERYDAY MEALS AND SNACKS

Kaffe Bord er Dekket, Vær så God (The table is ready, come and get it!) Gudrun brought just as much care and attention to everyday meals as she did to special occasions and company dinners. Every meal included all the trimmings—condiments and sauces, *flatbrød*, and always butter, sometimes served in pretty butter curls. We had many favorite meals: meatballs with lots of gravy, potatoes, lingonberries, peas, and carrot salad; Gudrun's famous chicken; her fish, swimming in butter; ham dinner with apricot gravy and creamed potatoes; leg of lamb with mint sauce; New England boiled dinner of smoked butt, steamed potatoes, and boiled cabbage. She gave the same tender, loving care to every dish and made every mealtime a happy time for sharing.

## *FROKOST:* THE BREAKFAST OF (SKI) CHAMPIONS

When she was a girl in the wintertime in the west of Norway, where the mountains meet the sea, Gudrun rose every morning long before the sun shone on the fjords. Getting to school through the deep snow was a thrill to a cross country skier. She and her siblings would trek through the snow as effortlessly as if they were taking a stroll on a spring day, all the while anticipating the stash of rolled pancakes filled with raspberry jam they would enjoy upon arriving. When she became a wife and mother, Gudrun retained the tradition of generous breakfasts, serving a wide variety of menus, always with milk, coffee, and orange juice. One day the family might sit down to French toast with bacon, sausage, or a variety of *spekemat* (paper-thin slices of dried meat, often mutton), dark bread and cheese, and grapefruit halves baked and glazed with brown sugar and a cherry on top. On another day, they'd breakfast on Gudrun's pancakes, piled high with syrup, sugar, butter, and fresh berries or melon, or scrambled eggs with blueberry or date-oatmeal muffins, toast, and sausage. Eddie's favorite way to eat pancakes was to spread the pancake all over with butter, sprinkle granulated sugar on it, then roll it up and start eating. Irving and the children delighted in these morning treats and headed off to their respective daily tasks full of energy and nutrients, a sweet taste lingering in their mouths.

# Gudrun's Crepes Suzette

*Crepes Suzette were often eaten with coffee or as a hurry-up snack when someone came to visit. Gudrun always cooked them in a well-seasoned cast-iron frying pan that had a gleaming smooth surface. This recipe serves two or three people for breakfast and four or five as a snack with coffee. A 6-inch pan will yield eight to ten crepes, and a 12-inch pan about four or five. This recipe multiplies well.*

    2 eggs
    1 cup half-and-half
    ½ cup all-purpose or cake flour
    2 tablespoons sugar
    2 tablespoons butter, melted
    2 teaspoons vanilla extract
    Pinch of salt
    Additional butter for preparing pan
    Jam or butter and sugar for serving

Beat eggs. Add remaining ingredients slowly, beating constantly until thoroughly mixed. The batter should be thin and pour easily; you may add more half-and-half if it is too thick.

Melt a little butter in a cast-iron pan over low to medium heat. Pour ⅛ to ¼ cup batter for a 6-inch pan, and ¼ cup for a 12-inch pan, tilting the pan so a thin layer of batter covers the entire surface. Let cook until you see bubbles start to form and the top starts to look firm. Using a spatula, carefully flip the crepe. Let cook another 30 seconds, until the other side is light tan. Slide the crepe out of the frying pan and spread it with a layer of strawberry or raspberry jam, or with butter and a sprinkling of sugar, and roll it up, to be eaten by hand or with a fork. Continue with remaining batter, adding a little butter to the pan before making each crepe.

# Gudrun's French Toast

*This recipe serves two but can easily be doubled or tripled. Gudrun used rich white bread, often homemade, about one-half inch thick. Serve with homemade jam or swimming in maple syrup.*

2 eggs
2 tablespoons milk or cream
1 tablespoon sugar
1 teaspoon vanilla extract
Pinch of salt
1 teaspoon nutmeg
¼ teaspoon cinnamon or apple pie spice
3 or 4 slices bread
Butter for frying
Jam or maple syrup

Beat eggs with a fork. Add milk or cream, sugar, vanilla extract, and salt. Sprinkle nutmeg and cinnamon or apple pie spice into mixture. One at a time, soak each slice of bread in mixture until the egg mixture has soaked throughout. Brown slices on both sides in a buttered frying pan and serve with jam or syrup.

# Gudrun's Pancakes

*Gudrun's pancakes should be served with butter and sugar sprinkled on top and piled high enough so that you can barely see over them when seated at the breakfast table. The pancakes should be cooked on a very hot skillet and removed only when the cook begins flirting with that line between perfection and burnt.*

> 1 tablespoon sugar
> 1 egg (Gudrun used jumbo eggs)
> 1 cup milk
> 1 cup pancake mix (such as Aunt Jemima),
>     all-purpose flour, or cake flour
> 1 tablespoon butter, melted
> 1 teaspoon vanilla extract
> Bacon
> Butter and sugar or maple syrup

Mix together sugar and egg. Alternating, add milk and flour or pancake mix 1 tablespoon at a time. Beat until smooth. Add melted butter and vanilla extract and mix well.

Using a 12-inch frying pan or cast-iron griddle, fry bacon and set aside, then pour off all but a small amount of fat. Pour in about ¼ cup of pancake batter (these are very thin) and cook over medium-high heat, until bubbles form and underside is golden brown, about 30 seconds. Flip the pancake and cook an additional 30 seconds. (You may choose to cook these thin pancakes at medium heat instead to prevent burning; allow about 1 minute for each side.)

Spread with butter, sprinkle with sugar, and roll up, or serve with maple syrup.

# Norwegian Coffee Waffles

*This rich batter can be used with a heart-shaped waffle iron, regular waffle iron, or Belgian waffle iron. For each batch, use enough batter to fill the iron without bubbling out when you close the top. (For heart-shaped waffles that is usually about ⅓ cup for the five hearts.)*

> 3 eggs, separated
> 1 cup milk or half-and-half
> ½ cup sugar
> 1 cup cake flour, sifted
> 2 tablespoons butter, melted
> 1 teaspoon vanilla extract
> ¼ teaspoon salt

Using an electric mixer, beat egg whites until stiff peaks form; set aside. In a separate bowl, beat egg yolks with a fork and add milk or half-and-half and sugar. Add cake flour to egg yolk mixture, then stir in melted butter, vanilla extract, and salt. Fold in egg whites. Pour about ⅓ cup to ½ cup batter into a waffle iron, depending on the size of the iron, so that the batter spreads over the entire iron but does not run over when you close the top. Cook 1 minute or until golden brown on both sides.

## THE HULLABALOO

In Gudrun's house, even snack time was a big to-do. Gudrun's grandson Erik recalls frequent childhood sleepovers with his brother Quinn at the home of their grandparents ("Gigi" and "Boppa"): "Gigi would ask Boppa if he would take us to Baskin-Robbins. 'Oh, Irving,' she would say, 'don't be a party pooper—take us to Packard & Rallins tonight!' With that they would laugh and laugh. She gave the ice cream shop a new name every time. If Boppa wouldn't take us to Baskin-Robbins, she would say, 'Oh, boys, don't worry about that old party pooper, we'll have a hullabaloo!'"

And a hullabaloo it was. The boys would sit down to a platter of snacks and desserts including Gudrun's famous chocolate chip cookies, spiced nuts, pinwheels of sliced peaches and orange segments (which she always called "orange booties"), sliced apples (sometimes with peanut butter), a crystal bowl full of carrot curls and celery sticks floating in ice water, plus sherbet, Neapolitan ice cream, and a delicious Danish junket that would stain their mouths bright red. To drink they'd have hot chocolate, a glass of milk, or Dr. Pepper, with ice cubes in the shapes of aces, clubs, diamonds, and hearts.

Irving even created a spinning snack wheel dartboard, each section of which bore a picture of a pear, an apple, a popsicle, and various other snacks. The boys would spin the wheel, shoot their dart gun at it, and whichever section their suction dart stuck on, that was the treat they got. Other times, Gudrun would exclaim, "Let's have an apple party!" and everyone came running.

# Homemade Hot Chocolate

½ cup boiling water
2 squares (1 ounce each) baking chocolate
3–4 cups whole, 2%, or skim milk
1 vanilla bean
½ cup granulated sugar
Marshmallows

Combine ½ cup boiling water and chocolate in the top of a double boiler set over simmering water. Stir until melted. In a separate pan, combine milk and vanilla bean. Heat the milk just to a boil to scald it, then turn down to a simmer (do not continue to boil). Add sugar and stir until dissolved. Whisk 1 cup of the hot scalded milk into the melted chocolate, then add that mixture to the remaining hot milk. Remove the vanilla bean before serving. Scoop with a ladle into cups and top with marshmallows.

# Spiced Nuts

1 cup granulated sugar

4 tablespoons water

2 teaspoons cinnamon

½ teaspoon ground cloves

½ teaspoon nutmeg

¼ teaspoon salt

¼ pound shelled nuts, such as
 walnuts, almonds, or filberts

Combine all ingredients except nuts and boil to the soft-ball stage. (The soft-ball stage is reached when a small amount of the syrup, dropped into cold water, forms a small, flexible ball.) Immediately add nuts to mixture, stirring quickly. When mixed well, pour mixture onto a flat surface such as a cutting board. Let cool before separating nuts.

## NATTMAT

*Nattmat* is the Norwegian equivalent of a midnight snack or a nightcap. When Gudrun and Irene were visiting Norway in 1963, *Tante* Ingeborg would come home late at night after a long day managing her hotel and cooking and overseeing the kitchen to make sure everything they served was perfect. She would bring with her a delicious array of *smørbrød* and desserts for *nattmat*, including *pariser* (*smørbrød* with seasoned ground beef) and *napoleonskaker*, a layered dessert made of pastry, custard, whipped cream, and frosting.

Upon entering Gudrun's home, no time was wasted before you were offered coffee, whether it was eight o'clock in the morning or in the middle of the night for *nattmat*. A visitor unaccustomed to Gudrun's brand of hospitality would be pleasantly surprised by a beautifully arranged platter of cookies and *smørbrød*, with a side of coffee, of course. A proper serving of coffee à la Gudrun must include an aesthetically pleasing arrangement of cheese, *smørbrød*, coffee waffles, cookies, and coffee cake.

# SMØRBRØD

*Smørbrød* are open-faced sandwiches made on thin slices of bread, buttered and trimmed of crusts, and topped decoratively with an endless array of ingredients including vegetables, cheese, eggs, fish, and meat.

Cheese (*ost*) is a must on the Norwegian table. For *smørbrød*, cheese is always presented as paper-thin shavings folded decoratively atop thin slices of buttered rye or dark bread and often topped with thinly sliced cucumber or pickle made into a curlicue. One should serve two or three kinds of cheese at a minimum, at least one soft and one hard variety. Olives, thin slides of radish or radish roses, and celery provide an ideal garnish. Butter, crackers, pumpernickel, and rye, French, or whole-grain dark bread should accompany it.

Some of the most common cheeses are *nøkkelost* (a semihard cow's milk cheese spiced with cumin, caraway, and clove), *bonde ost* (a soft yellow cheese), Edam, Emmental, Swiss, Gouda, Jarlsberg, Gorgonzola, French Port Salut, *gjetost*, and *gammelost*. The two we enjoyed the most were *gammelost* and *gjetost*. *Gammelost*, which translates as "old cheese," is a pungent traditional Norwegian cheese that was once a staple of the Norwegian diet. It looks something like blue cheese but has a completely different character. Like many traditional Norwegian foods, such as flat bread, dried, salted, and smoked meats, and stockfish, *gammelost* could be stored for long periods without refrigeration. In the days when young girls spent summers in the mountains of Norway, *gammelost* was made each June. Skim milk was allowed to sour in a wooden bucket. It was then heated in a large cast-iron pot. When the curds separated, they were placed in a wooden form lined with cheesecloth to drain the liquid. The drained cheese was placed on a warm shelf in the *saeter* hut and taken down to the farm with the animals in the fall. By Christmas, the cheese had fermented to a brown color and was ready to eat. *Gammelost* was reported to prevent sickness and infection; some say you can eat *gammelost* instead of taking penicillin.

It was a supreme treat for Irving when he was able to get *gammelost* from a Chicago delicatessen. (Once Irene found it in Washington, D.C., and sent him an entire wheel.) He'd spread just a little pungent cheese on a thin slice of dark bread, rye, wheat, or *flatbrød*, a traditional Norwegian unleavened bread. *Gammelost* smelled so bad that it had a home on the back porch, in a sealed container!

*Gjetost* (pronounced "yet-oast"), also called *brunost* (brown cheese), is best served in wafer-thin slices, cut by an *ostehøvel* (Norwegian cheese knife), of course, on *flatbrød* or thin sliced rye or wheat bread. It is as commonly associated with Norway as trolls and fjords. Legend says that more than one hundred years ago on a small summer farm high above Gudbrandsdalen Valley, a milkmaid had just made the curd from cow's and goat's milk. The leftover whey was boiling in a great iron kettle in the fireplace. Usually she would allow almost all the liquid to evaporate, leaving a golden paste at the bottom of the kettle to be used for sandwich spread. One night, she expected visitors and wanted to serve them something special, so she added cream and goat's milk and poured the hot mixture into a mold. That night she probably served the first golden *gjetost* ever made.

## Gjetost

To make your own *gjetost*, pour 1 gallon fresh goat's milk whey into a large heavy-bottomed pot. Bring to boil over high heat, stirring often so it doesn't stick. Lower the heat and simmer uncovered for as many hours as needed to reduce the volume. When the consistency has become more viscous (about 5 to 6 hours), begin to watch closely, stirring regularly to prevent burning or sticking. When the consistency resembles fudge, remove *gjetost* from heat, whisk vigorously, and pour into an ice-cold buttered pan to cool rapidly. Keep refrigerated.

In our household, the only way to cut properly thin slices of cheese was with a Norwegian cheese slicer called an *ostehøvel*. My father's family had contests to see who could cut a paper-thin slice of cheese and still leave the top of the block flat.

The *ostehøvel* has been a national icon and a fixture in every kitchen since it was invented and patented by Thor Bjørklund in 1925. According to the Norwegian patent office, one hot summer day, Bjørklund took a break in his carpenter workshop in Lillehammer to enjoy the lunch his wife had prepared: four slices of bread with Gouda cheese. However, the summer heat had caused his cheese to melt uninvitingly. He tried to divide the slices of cheese into more appetizing thin slices, first using a knife, then a saw. Finally, he tried the plane he had been using to slice wood. He got the thin slices he'd hoped for, though the tool was still a bit too large and difficult to use. After thinking about this overnight, Bjørklund cut and bent a thin piece of steel so that a nice slice of cheese could slip right off the blade and through the back. Neighbors and friends loved his invention, and soon he realized that he should take out a patent for his product.

Cheese is only one possible topping for *smørbrød*. There is an endless variety, all beginning with bread sliced as thinly as possible and buttered, then spread to each edge with filling, trimmed of its crusts, and cut, slantwise, into two or three narrow pieces. *Smørbrød* toppings should be layered, folded, or arranged decoratively, and the sandwiches are generally topped with garnishes such as twists of lemon, cucumber, or rosettes of mayonnaise.

# Homemade Mayonnaise I

*Gudrun made her own mayonnaise to serve with her* smørbrød, *but purchased mayonnaise works as well. This recipe contains uncooked egg yolks, which can be a health concern. A recipe with cooked egg yolks follows.*

> 1 teaspoon dry mustard
> 1 teaspoon salt
> 1 teaspoon confectioners' sugar
> 2 egg yolks
> 2 tablespoons vinegar, divided
> 1½ cups olive oil, chilled
> 2 tablespoons lemon juice

Combine mustard, salt, and sugar in a medium bowl. Add the egg yolks and mix well with an electric mixer or whisk. Blend in ½ teaspoon vinegar. Add some of the oil in a gradual drizzle, stirring constantly. Alternating, continue adding oil, then vinegar and lemon juice, a little at a time, until all of it is used and the mayonnaise is emulsified and thick enough to spread on *smørbrød*. If the mixture thickens too much, thin with a little vinegar. Refrigerate mayonnaise in a sterilized glass jar or any container with a tight cover.

## Homemade Mayonnaise II

*This version, made with cooked eggs, is based on Gudrun's version and an adaptation from* Farm Recipes and Food Secrets from the Norske Nook *by Helen Myhre and Mona Vold. It makes about 1 cup. If you would like to mimic the flavor of Miracle Whip, add the optional teaspoon of sugar, as Gudrun did.*

> 1 tablespoon butter
> 2 tablespoons flour
> ½ cup water
> 1 egg yolk, well beaten
> ½ teaspoon dry mustard
> ½ teaspoon salt
> Dash of paprika
> 1 teaspoon sugar (optional)
> 1 tablespoon vinegar
> ½ cup peanut or safflower oil

In a heavy skillet over low heat, melt the butter and stir in the flour using a wooden spoon to make a roux. Add the water and cook until sauce is thick and white.

Add the beaten egg yolk, dry mustard, salt, paprika, and sugar if using, and cook mixture until smooth, stirring constantly. Place the vinegar in a medium mixing bowl, add the cooked ingredients, and beat with an electric mixer on medium speed. Add the oil 1 teaspoon at a time, blending until all the oil is incorporated. Refrigerate mayonnaise in a sterilized glass jar or any container with a tight cover.

# Tomato and Cheese *Smørbrød*

> Butter
> White or dark bread, thinly sliced
> Ripe tomatoes, sliced
> Salt and pepper to taste
> Whipped butter, seasoned with dill, thyme, or garlic
> Jarlsberg, Cheddar, or Gruyère cheese, grated fine

Butter bread and cut off the crusts. Add a slice of ripe tomato. Season with salt and pepper and add a rosette of whipped, seasoned butter. Sprinkle the sandwich with grated cheese.

# Tomato and Egg *Smørbrød*

> Butter
> White or dark bread, thinly sliced
> Hard-cooked eggs, sliced horizontally
> Ripe tomatoes
> Chopped basil or salt and pepper to taste

Butter and trim bread and layer with rings of hard-cooked egg. Top each with a thin slice of seasoned ripe tomato with a little fresh basil or salt and pepper.

## Butter and Chive *Smørbrød*

> Butter, softened
> Minced chives
> French bread, sliced

Whip butter until light, adding enough minced chives to give it color and flavor. Spread on slices of fresh French bread. Do not trim crust.

## Carrot and Pea *Smørbrød*

> Butter
> White or dark bread, thinly sliced
> Cooked carrots, thinly sliced
> Cooked peas
> Cooked cauliflower, chopped fine
> Salt and pepper to taste
> Whipped butter or mayonnaise

Butter bread and trim crusts. Cover each slice of bread with carrots and garnish with very small peas and cauliflower. Season with salt and pepper and add a dab or rosette of whipped butter or mayonnaise.

# Celery and Radish *Smørbrød*

*Irving loved* smørbrød *with sliced radish or thinly sliced Spanish onions.*

> Butter
> White bread, thinly sliced
> Radishes, sliced very thin but not pared
> Celery, sliced or chopped
> Salt and pepper to taste
> Whipped butter or mayonnaise

Butter bread and trim crusts. Layer bread with radish and celery and season with salt and pepper. Leave plain or garnish with whipped butter or mayonnaise.

# Cream Cheese and Vegetable *Smørbrød*

> Butter
> White or rye bread, thinly sliced, or *flatbrød*, or
>    Wasabröd (a cracker-like crispbread)
> Cream cheese
> Lettuce
> Thinly sliced white onion, cucumber, or radishes

Butter bread. Spread thinly with cream cheese and top with lettuce. Finish with white onion, cucumber, or radishes, thinly sliced and slit almost through the diameter, then decoratively twisted.

## Smoked Salmon and Scrambled Egg *Smørbrød*

Butter
White or rye bread, thinly sliced
Scrambled eggs
Smoked salmon
Fresh dill
Lemon

Butter bread and trim crusts. Pile a spoonful of scrambled egg on each slice of bread. Lay one or two slices of smoked salmon on top, cut to fit the bread. Sprinkle fresh dill on top and garnish with a thinly sliced lemon, cut from the center out and twisted.

## Pickled Herring and Egg *Smørbrød*

Butter
White bread, pumpernickel, or rye, thinly sliced
Hard-cooked eggs, sliced horizontally
Pickled herring
Mayonnaise
Paprika

Butter bread and trim crusts. Layer with rings of hard-cooked egg. Top with one chunk of herring fillet and finish with a twirl of mayonnaise out of a tube and a sprinkle of paprika.

# Sardine or Mackerel and Egg *Smørbrød*

Butter
White bread, thinly sliced
Hard-cooked eggs, sliced horizontally
Sardines or mackerel
Mayonnaise
Paprika
Sliced tomato

Butter bread and trim crusts. Layer rings of hard-cooked egg and crisscross two sardines or pieces of mackerel on top. Garnish with a twirl of thick mayonnaise out of a tube and a sprinkle of paprika, then add a thin wedge of tomato on top.

# Salad Shrimp *Smørbrød*

Mayonnaise
Lemon juice
Cocktail sauce
Butter
White bread, thinly sliced
Salad shrimp
Parsley

Combine mayonnaise, lemon juice, and cocktail sauce to taste—for a lemony version, use a ratio of 1 tablespoon mayonnaise, 1 teaspoon fresh lemon juice, and 1 tablespoon cocktail sauce.

Butter bread, trim crusts, and spread with mayonnaise mixture. Top with a scant ¼ cup shrimp and add another dollop of mayonnaise mixture on top. Squeeze lemon juice on top and finish with a parsley leaf.

# Anchovy and Egg *Smørbrød*

*This sandwich must be eaten with a knife and fork.*

> Butter
> White or rye bread, thinly sliced
> Hard-cooked eggs, sliced horizontally
> Anchovy fillets, cleaned and boned, and halved lengthwise
> Minced parsley

Butter bread, layer with rings of hard-cooked egg, and trim crusts. Use anchovy fillets as border or crisscrossed. Garnish with finely minced parsley.

# Shrimp and Mayonnaise *Smørbrød*

> Butter
> Loaf French bread, sliced thinly into rounds
> Minced and seasoned cooked shrimp
> Mayonnaise
> Minced lettuce

Spread French bread with butter; do not trim crust. Place shrimp around the edge of each round; fill the center with mayonnaise. Add garnish of minced lettuce.

# Pickled Herring *Smørbrød*

*You may serve this herring unadorned or with sour cream on bread, crackers, or flatbrød. Allow time for fish to soak overnight and for the completed dish to rest for a few hours or overnight.*

> 3 large salt-preserved herring
> 1 cup vinegar
> ½ cup sugar
> ½ cup finely chopped white onions
> 12 whole allspice
> 3 bay leaves
> 2 or 3 sprigs fresh dill
> Pepper

Cover the herring with cold water and let them stand overnight. Drain, split, and skin them, removing all bones. Cut each fillet horizontally in eight narrow strips, then slide a knife or a spatula under each cut fillet, keeping slices together, and place in a flat dish. Mix all other ingredients and pour over the herring. Let stand overnight, or at least for several hours before serving.

# Smoked Herring and Egg *Smørbrød*

Smoked herring, cleaned, boned, and soaked
    overnight in cold water
Butter
White bread, thinly sliced
Hard-cooked egg yolks, grated
Hard-cooked egg whites, chopped fine
Minced lettuce

Drain herring and wipe dry. Mince or shred the herring very fine. On thin, buttered slices of bread, alternate strips of minced herring, egg yolk, and egg white. Trim crusts and garnish with minced lettuce.

# Salami and Cucumber *Smørbrød*

Butter
White bread, rye, or pumpernickel, thinly sliced
Hard salami
Cucumber or pickle

Butter bread. Place thin slices of hard salami, folded over decoratively, on each slice of bread. Top with a thinly sliced pickle or a twist of thinly sliced cucumber.

# Pariser (*Smørbrød* with Seasoned Ground Beef)

*This sandwich is also good with a little sautéed onion: brown sliced onions in butter with a teaspoon of sugar and top each sandwich with it. Serves 4.*

> 1 pound round steak, ground in a meat grinder
>     or chopped in a food processor
> 2 tablespoons cream or undiluted evaporated milk
> 1 small onion, grated fine (juice and pulp)
> 1 teaspoon red wine vinegar
> ¾ teaspoon Worcestershire sauce
> ¼ teaspoon pepper
> ¼ teaspoon crushed thyme
> 1 egg, beaten
> 1 small handful of capers
> Butter
> 4 slices rye bread with caraway seeds, grilled or toasted

Mix together all ingredients except butter and bread. Form into four patties. Melt butter in a frying pan and brown patties well. Serve patties, with drippings from pan, on slices of grilled or toasted rye bread with caraway seeds.

# Salads

## ☙ Fruit Salads

Apple Pineapple Celery Salad

Frozen Cranberry Salad

Mandarin Orange Salad

Orange Jell-O Salad

## ☙ Vegetable Salads

Bean Salad

Carrot Salad

Cabbage Salad with Sour Cream Dressing

Cucumber Salad

Norwegian Potato Salad

Tomato Swiss Salad

## ☙ Salads with Meat and Fish

Chicken Salad

Curried Turkey Salad

Seafood Salad

Chilled and Molded *Sillsallad* (Herring Salad)

*Sillsallad*

## FRUIT SALADS

# Apple Pineapple Celery Salad

*This crunchy salad serves 8 to 10.*

> 3 cups diced apples
> 2 cups diced celery
> 1 can (14 ounces) crushed pineapple, drained, reserving 1 cup juice
> ⅓ cup sugar
> ¼ cup water
> 1 tablespoon cornstarch
> Lettuce cups
> ½ cup crushed English walnuts

Combine apples, celery, and drained pineapple in a serving bowl. In a small saucepan, combine reserved pineapple juice, sugar, water, and cornstarch and cook until clear. Cool. Pour over fruit and mix well. Serve in lettuce cups and sprinkle walnuts on top.

# Frozen Cranberry Salad

*Make this salad a few hours ahead to allow time for freezing. Serves 6 to 8 as an accompaniment to pot roast, stew, chicken, or roasted turkey.*

> 1 can (14–16 ounces) whole cranberry sauce
> 1 can (8 ounces) crushed pineapple
> 1 cup sour cream

Mix all ingredients in a medium-sized bowl. Line a 6 x 9-inch or 8 x 8-inch pan with waxed paper or parchment paper. Spread salad in pan. Depending on size of pan, the salad will be one or two inches thick. Place in freezer for at least 2 hours or until frozen. Serve frozen, cut into squares or rectangles.

# Mandarin Orange Salad

*Gudrun served this salad with pot roast, roast pork, baked chicken breast, or baked salmon.*

> 1 cup baby marshmallows
> 1 cup mandarin oranges, drained
> 1 cup pineapple chunks, drained
> 1 cup coconut
> 1 cup sour cream

Mix all ingredients in a large bowl. Cover and chill in refrigerator. Serve cold.

# Orange Jell-O Salad

> 2 packages (3 ounces each) orange Jell-O
> 1½ cups boiling water
> 1 can (20 ounces) crushed pineapple, drained, juice reserved
> 1 can (11 ounces) mandarin oranges, drained, juice reserved
> 1 pint orange sherbet

Dissolve orange Jell-O in 1½ cups boiling water. Add reserved juice from the pineapple and oranges. Stir in orange sherbet to melt. Let mixture cool in refrigerator to thicken a little. Then add fruit and pour into ring mold. Refrigerate till firm.

## VEGETABLE SALADS

# Bean Salad

*This salad is served chilled. Allow a couple of hours to refrigerate.*

> 5 cups cooked beans (such as a mix of kidney,
>   pinto, green, garbanzo, and black beans)
> ½ cup chopped scallions
> ½ cup minced red onion
> ¼ cup chopped fresh parsley
> 3 cloves garlic, crushed
> Juice from ½ large lemon (1½–2 tablespoons)
> ¾ cup combined olive oil and safflower oil
> ½ cup vinegar
> 1 tablespoon dry red wine
> ½ teaspoon basil
> ½ teaspoon salt
> Fresh black pepper to taste
> Pinch of marjoram or oregano

Briefly sauté beans, scallions, onion, and parsley and place in large serving bowl. In a separate bowl, mix together remaining ingredients and pour over bean mixture. Combine and chill at least 2 hours or overnight.

# Carrot Salad

*The carrots and onions in this dish must be very, very finely shredded. Gudrun's grater somehow resulted in just the right consistency. Store-bought grated carrots or those grated in a Cuisinart result in too coarse a shred, but we've found that an OXO grater provides the right texture. This salad is lovely served molded on a bed of greens or straight from the bowl in which it was chilled and set. We often serve it with baked ham, a meatball dinner, or a leg of lamb at Easter. The recipe makes four generous servings; we usually at least double it because we love it so much.*

> 1 package (3 ounces) orange Jell-O
> 1 cup boiling water
> ½ cup cold water
> 1 tablespoon mayonnaise
> 2 cups finely grated carrots (about 5 large carrots)
> 2 teaspoons finely grated onion
> 1 teaspoon salt

In a large bowl add the boiling water to the Jell-O and stir until dissolved. Then add the cold water. Let the Jell-O cool about 15 minutes, either at room temperature or in the refrigerator, so it is slightly firm but not gelled. Add mayonnaise and mix well. When Jell-O is cool, add carrots, onion, and salt and mix thoroughly. Pour the mixture into a mold or a bowl and let it gel in the refrigerator.

# Cabbage Salad with Sour Cream Dressing

*This makes a lightly dressed salad. If you like more dressing, use half a head of cabbage or lettuce, or double the dressing ingredients.*

    1 head white cabbage or iceberg lettuce
    ½ cup sour cream
    2 tablespoons vinegar
    2 tablespoons sugar
    ½ teaspoon salt
    Pinch of paprika

Finely shred or chop cabbage or lettuce. Place in a large bowl. In a smaller bowl, blend all other ingredients with a fork or whisk until smooth. Serve drizzled over lettuce or cabbage, or toss to blend.

# Cucumber Salad

*This salad keeps well in the refrigerator for several days. It is best made with European cucumbers or just-harvested regular cucumbers. Allow time for cucumbers to chill and for dressing ingredients to marry.*

3 medium cucumbers, or
   3 long European cucumbers
Salt

**Dressing**
1 cup white vinegar
4–8 tablespoons sugar, to taste
1 tablespoon water
1 tablespoon salt
2½ teaspoons minced fresh dill or
   1 teaspoon dried dill (or less, to taste)
¾ teaspoon black pepper

Peel the cucumbers and slice them paper-thin using a vegetable peeler or *ostehøvel*. (If the cucumber has a lot of big seeds, slice it lengthwise first and scoop the seeds out with a spoon.) Place the slices in a flat bowl or plate, sprinkle with salt, and mix, turning cucumbers over in the salt. Place a smaller plate on top of the cucumbers that can be pressed down into the bowl or plate. Allow this to stand about 1 hour in the refrigerator. Drain the juice from the cucumbers.

To make the dressing, combine the vinegar, sugar to taste, water, salt, dill, and pepper in a small bowl. Stir well with a fork and pour over the cucumbers. Allow this to stand 30 minutes or longer in the refrigerator.

**Variation:** For a slightly different flavor and darker color, replace the white vinegar with ½ cup cider vinegar, replace the black pepper with white pepper, and add 1 tablespoon grated onion.

# Norwegian Potato Salad

*This delicious recipe serves 6 as a side dish with baked ham or ribs, but it is also great for a crowd—we double or triple the recipe for Christmas parties and other events. Red Bliss or Yukon Gold potatoes work well, but new potatoes from the black dirt in Minnesota and the North Dakota Red River valley are the best. The salad will need to chill for 4 to 6 hours before serving.*

6 large, firm potatoes (enough for about 6 cups cubed potatoes)
16 slices of bacon
2 cups chopped celery
1 onion, grated or chopped fine
2–3 teaspoons chopped parsley
2 eggs, beaten
¼ cup sugar
¼ cup white vinegar

¼ cup tarragon vinegar
1½ teaspoons salt
⅛ teaspoon pepper
⅛ teaspoon powdered savory
¼ cup cold water
½ teaspoon dry mustard
6–8 cups salad greens, chilled
4 tomatoes, cut in wedges
1 cucumber, sliced thin

Steam or boil the potatoes whole with the skins on for 20 to 30 minutes, until they are easy to pierce with a fork but not yet soft. They should be cooked through and firm. After the potatoes cool, peel off the thin skin by rubbing it with a knife blade or, if desired, leave the skin on.

While the potatoes are cooking, fry bacon in a skillet until crisp. Remove and drain bacon on paper towels or paper bag. Pour off all but ¼ cup of skillet drippings. Crumble bacon and set aside.

Cut potatoes into 1-inch pieces. In a large bowl, toss together the potatoes, celery, onion, parsley, and crumbled bacon and set aside.

In a separate bowl, mix eggs, sugar, white vinegar, tarragon vinegar, salt, pepper, and savory.

In another small bowl, blend water and dry mustard to make a smooth paste. Add mustard mixture to egg mixture and pour egg mixture into drippings in skillet. Cook over low heat, stirring, until thick and smooth. Add to potato mixture and combine thoroughly. Cover and chill 4 to 6 hours or overnight. Serve on top of salad greens and garnish with tomatoes. Place thin cucumber slices in overlapping rings on top or in a circle around the edge of the bowl.

## Tomato Swiss Salad

> 3 hard-cooked eggs, chopped
> ¼ pound thinly sliced Swiss cheese,
>     cut into small pieces
> ¼ cup chopped green bell pepper
> ½ teaspoon horseradish
> ¼ teaspoon salt
> ⅛ teaspoon pepper
> ½ cup sour cream
> 8 tomato slices
> 4 lettuce cups
> Sliced hard-cooked egg for garnish (optional)

Gently toss together chopped eggs, Swiss cheese, and green pepper. In a separate bowl, fold horseradish, salt, and pepper into sour cream. Gently combine with egg mixture.

Arrange tomato slices in lettuce cups. Mound egg mixture on tomato slices. Garnish with hard-cooked egg slices if desired.

## SALADS WITH MEAT AND FISH

# Chicken Salad

*This is a good way to use leftover baked chicken.*

> 3 cups finely chopped or shredded cooked chicken
> 1 cup finely chopped celery
> ½ cup mayonnaise or Miracle Whip
> ½ cup halved seedless grapes
> 3 tablespoons cream
> 2 tablespoons lemon juice
> 2 tablespoons shredded carrots
> ½ teaspoon salt
> Shredded iceberg or romaine lettuce, spinach,
>     or other field greens
> Sliced tomatoes or tomato wedges
> Hard-cooked eggs
> Slivered or sliced almonds (optional)

Mix chicken, celery, mayonnaise, grapes, cream, lemon juice, carrots, and salt thoroughly. Serve over a bed of greens, surrounded by tomato slices or wedges and hard-cooked eggs for decoration. You can also add slivered or sliced almonds if you like.

# Curried Turkey Salad

*This hearty, main dish salad makes 6 small servings, great for a lunch. Double the ingredients for 6 dinner servings.*

>1 cup cooked rice
>1 tablespoon vegetable oil
>2 teaspoons vinegar
>½ teaspoon salt
>½ teaspoon curry powder
>1 cup cubed cooked turkey
>1 cup cooked green peas
>¼ cup chopped celery
>2 tablespoons chopped green or red bell pepper
>⅓ cup bottled or homemade vinaigrette
>2 sliced fresh peaches or 1 can (16 ounces) peaches,
>    sliced and drained
>Minced parsley

Mix cooked rice with vegetable oil, vinegar, salt, and curry powder. Just before serving, combine rice mixture with turkey, peas, celery, and bell pepper and toss with vinaigrette. Garnish with sliced peaches and parsley.

# Seafood Salad

*Gudrun always served this salad in a crystal bowl lined with shredded lettuce and surrounded decoratively with tomato wedges and hard-cooked eggs, either diced or cut in quarters. A bowl of carrot curls, radish roses, and celery sticks with ice cubes on top to keep the vegetables crisp completed the meal. She also served this with individual side dishes of sliced canned pineapple rings with cottage cheese in the center. Serves 4 with rolls, dark bread, flat bread, or sourdough.*

3 or 4 hard-cooked eggs, chopped
 or cut into wedges
2 cans (7 ounces each) tuna, shrimp,
 crab, or salmon, drained
2 cups sliced or finely diced celery
1 cup Miracle Whip or mayonnaise
1 can (15 ounces) baby peas, drained, or
 a small package of frozen baby peas
¼ large onion, grated, or 1 teaspoon
 onion salt or dried onion
1 tablespoon lemon juice
A few dashes Tabasco or other
 hot pepper sauce (optional)
Diced cucumbers (optional)
1 cup sliced crisp lettuce, such as iceberg or romaine
Sliced cucumbers, radish roses, tomato slices, or
 diced or quartered hard-cooked eggs for garnish

Gently mix together all ingredients except lettuce and garnish. Place salad in a bowl and surround with sliced lettuce. (You can also serve the salad on top of a bed of sliced lettuce.) Decorate on top with cucumber slices scored with a fork, radish roses, hard-cooked eggs, and tomato slices.

# Chilled and Molded *Sillsallad* (Herring Salad)

*Use jarred pickled herring or buy long whole fillets from a kosher deli. The salad will need to refrigerate for a few hours to set. Serves 8 to 10 people.*

Salad oil for preparing the mold
4 small herring fillets, cut into 1-inch cubes
4 cups diced boiled potatoes, such as red or Yukon Gold
1½ cups diced beets, raw, pickled, or cooked
1 cup diced carrots
1 cup diced apples
⅔ cup diced onion

**Dressing**
½ cup white vinegar
¼ cup water
¼ cup sugar
¼ teaspoon salt
Dash of white pepper
Chopped parsley and 2 hard-cooked eggs, cut into wedges

Rinse a 5-cup mold with cold water, wipe it dry, and brush lightly with salad oil. Mix chopped herring fillets with potatoes, beets, carrots, apples, and onions.

In another bowl, blend vinegar, water, sugar, salt, and pepper. Stir gently into salad. Pack salad into prepared 5-cup mold. Chill in the refrigerator for a few hours. Unmold salad onto a serving platter and garnish with chopped parsley and egg wedges.

# *Sillsallad*

6 new potatoes
¼ cup French dressing
2 apples, diced
1 jar (5 ounces) pickled herring, drained and cut small
3 hard-cooked eggs, chopped
⅓ cup mayonnaise or Miracle Whip
¼ teaspoon dried tarragon
Salt and pepper to taste
1 can (15 ounces) diced beets, drained
1 tablespoon capers

Boil the potatoes in their jackets until tender and then drain. When cool enough to handle, peel, dice, and drizzle lightly with the French dressing. Let cool.

Add apples, herring, hard-cooked eggs, mayonnaise, and tarragon. Mix well and season to taste with salt and pepper. Just before serving, stir in the drained beets and garnish with capers.

# Vegetables and Sides

Baked Beans

Chilled Bean Dip

Corn Ring

Creamed Green Peas

Creamed Onions

Creamed Potatoes

Curried Rice and Lentils

*Klubb* (Potato Dumplings)

*Blodklubb* (Blood Potato Dumplings)

*Latkes*

Stuffed Cabbage Rolls

*Surkål* (Sweet and Sour Cabbage)

# SUMMERTIME AND FRESH VEGETABLES

In the summertime, we always looked forward to fresh vegetables, from corn dinners to fresh peas. For corn dinners, my brother and I would sit out on the back steps, shucking the corn ears, being sure to remove all the corn silk. Then my mother would boil a big pot of water with a tablespoon of salt in it. She cooked the ears for 10 minutes, not too long, as the corn was so fresh—right from the fields. Then we would all sit down for dinner around the kitchen table. We would rub butter on the corn, sprinkle with salt, and eat our way around the ear of corn. Each of us wanted to see who could eat the most. The cobs piled up in a bowl on the table—we would eat seven or eight ears apiece. My mother often served this with a salad of pineapple rings and cottage cheese, or cole slaw. Sometimes she also had thin slices of bread, with thin hard salami.

My brother and I were also in charge of shelling peas. We would sit out on the back steps and take the fresh peas out of the pods, eating some of them raw as we went along. My mother would steam them for 3 or 4 minutes and then add a big pat of butter. Sometimes she would serve the peas in a special white cream sauce. Delicious.

My mother's favorite potatoes were the new potatoes from Minnesota, straight out of the ground. She steamed them and served them with butter and fresh chopped parsley on top. We then mashed them up with our forks in the sauces and gravies from the main course.

During World War II, as most families did in those days, we had a victory garden. The carrots and potatoes we grew in the backyard on East Street were out of this world. My mother always had a crystal bowl of freshly peeled carrot curls and celery, sitting in cold water and ice to keep them fresh, ready for snacks, dinner, or lunch. On Riverside Drive, we had wild fresh asparagus, rhubarb, strawberries growing in strawberry barrels, apple trees, and tomatoes. My mother canned the vegetables and made jams and jellies and pickles. We would smell baking bread and biscuits as we played outside, and I remember running into the house and coming out with fresh hot homemade bread with homemade jam or jelly. —Irene

# Baked Beans

*Serves 6 people as a side dish.*

> 1 pound Swedish brown beans, soaked
>     overnight and drained
> 2 small onions, chopped
> 2 cloves garlic
> 1 bay leaf
> ½ cup ketchup
> 3 tablespoons molasses
> 1 teaspoon dry mustard
> ½ teaspoon ground ginger
> ½ teaspoon salt
> ½ pound smoked bacon, diced
> ¼ cup brown sugar

Place beans in a large pot, cover with water, and bring to a boil. Boil for 5 minutes, then turn heat to low, cover the pot, and let simmer 1 hour. Add onions, garlic, and bay leaf to beans and cook until beans are tender, 1 to 2 hours. Drain, reserving 2½ cups of the liquid.

Preheat oven to 275 degrees. To bean liquid add ketchup, molasses, dry mustard, ground ginger, and salt. Place the beans in a bean pot, stir in bacon, add seasoned liquid, and sprinkle with brown sugar. Bake for 4 hours.

# Chilled Bean Dip

*A relative of the kidney bean, Jacob's Cattle beans are purple and white and are also called trout or coach beans. For this recipe you can substitute kidney beans. This dip is delicious served with corn chips.*

> 1½ cups Jacob's Cattle beans, cooked
> 2 or more fresh green chiles or jalapeño
>     peppers, chopped fine
> 1 tablespoon vinegar
> 1 teaspoon chili powder
> ⅛ teaspoon cumin
> 2 teaspoons minced onion
> 2 teaspoons minced parsley or cilantro

Place beans, peppers, vinegar, chili powder, and cumin in a blender and process until smooth. Transfer mixture to a serving bowl and stir in onion and parsley or cilantro.

# Corn Ring

> 2 eggs, beaten
> ½ cup milk
> 1 can (15.25 ounces) corn, drained
> ½ green pepper, diced
> Dash of salt

Preheat oven to 300 degrees. Mix together eggs and milk. Add corn, green pepper, and salt. Pour mixture into a well-oiled Bundt pan or 8-inch-square glass baking dish and bake until firm, 45 minutes to 1 hour.

# Creamed Green Peas

*We loved creamed peas, creamed dried beef, and other creamed vegetables—on toast, bread, or mashed potatoes. Each summer we'd sit on the back porch and open the pods, putting some of the peas in the bowl and many more in our mouths.*

2 cups fresh or frozen peas
4 tablespoons (½ stick) butter
2 tablespoons flour
1 cup whole milk plus more
    for thinning sauce if needed
1 teaspoon salt
½ teaspoon pepper
1 teaspoon nutmeg (optional)

Simmer the peas in 1 cup of water for 5 minutes. Drain, reserving 1 cup of the cooking liquid, and set aside.

Melt the butter in a small saucepan over medium heat. Slowly whisk in the flour and stir 3 to 5 minutes, until the flour taste is gone. Slowly add milk, continuing to stir, and bring mixture to a boil. Add salt and pepper. Add nutmeg, if using. Add more milk if the sauce gets too thick. Stir in the peas and serve.

**Variation:** Try this simpler version with freshly shelled peas. Place 2 cups fresh shelled peas or frozen peas in a heavy pan. Add water to cover and 1 teaspoon salt. Cook peas for about 10 minutes. Drain the peas, reserving the liquid. Add 2 tablespoons butter. Add 1 cup warmed half-and-half or cream and a little of the reserved cooking water if it seems too thick. Season with salt and pepper to taste and 1 teaspoon nutmeg if you like.

# Creamed Onions

*We always had creamed onions with Thanksgiving turkey. To make this ahead of time, follow the recipe through making the cream sauce. Then pour the cream sauce over onions in a casserole or glass dish and refrigerate it, covered, until you need it. Bake for 30 minutes at 350 degrees.*

2 pounds small white onions (1½–2 inches in diameter.
    You can use small onions in a can or jar if your store's
    produce department does not have the small onions.)
1 chicken bouillon cube
½ teaspoon salt
4 tablespoons (½ stick) butter
4 tablespoons flour
Pinch of salt
2 cups milk
½ cup heavy cream
Pinch of paprika

Pour boiling water over onions to cover and let stand 1 to 2 minutes. Drain and cover with cold water. Cut away top and bottom of each onion, removing as little as possible. Peel off outer skin and first onion layer. With the tip of a knife, pierce the root ends twice, forming a cross.

Place onions in a large saucepan, add chicken bouillon cube and ½ teaspoon salt and cover generously with boiling water. Cook, uncovered, until tender all through, about 30 minutes.

In the meantime, make the cream sauce. Melt butter in the top of a double boiler and whisk in flour until smooth. Continue whisking while cooking for 5 to 10 minutes. Season to taste with salt and keep hot.

Drain onions thoroughly. Slowly stir milk and cream into butter-flour mixture. Heat through, and pour sauce over onions. Sprinkle with paprika and serve.

# Creamed Potatoes

*These are best served with ham or fish dishes. This recipe will serve 8 people if the potatoes are big, but we usually double the recipe. The leftovers are delicious warmed up in a double boiler.*

8 russet potatoes
3–4 tablespoons butter
2 tablespoons flour
3–4 cups milk
1 teaspoon nutmeg or less, to taste
Salt to taste

Peel potatoes, cut into 1-inch chunks, and submerge in cold water until needed. Melt butter in the top of a double boiler. Turn heat to low and stir in flour. Cook about 5 minutes on low heat, then add milk gradually, stirring constantly, until mixture thickens to a cream sauce. Add nutmeg (just enough so you can see the flecks) and salt to taste. Drain potatoes, add to sauce, and simmer until heated through.

# Curried Rice and Lentils

*If you like curry and want more of it in this recipe, use as much as 1 tablespoon of good Indian curry powder. Then add more garnishes, such as yogurt, finely chopped green onions, and chopped fresh tomatoes.*

> 2 cups lentils, washed and sorted
> 2 cups brown rice
> 2 medium chopped onions
> 1 can (14 ounces) whole, stewed,
>    or diced tomatoes
> 1 can (4 ounces) tomato sauce
> 1 bay leaf
> ¼ teaspoon garlic powder
> ¼–1 teaspoon curry powder, to taste
> Raisins and chopped bananas for garnish

Bring 6 cups of water to a boil, add lentils, and let simmer on low heat for 1 hour or until lentils are tender. Drain lentils and set aside.

Bring 6 cups of water to a boil and add rice. Let boil for 1 minute, then lower heat, cover, and simmer on low for 25 minutes. Add lentils to rice along with onions, tomatoes, tomato sauce, bay leaf, garlic powder, and curry powder. Heat through on low heat for 10 minutes. Break up the tomatoes a bit with a spoon. Serve with raisins and chopped bananas on the side.

# *Klubb* (Potato Dumplings)

*We always knew Tante Borghild was coming to visit when we saw our mother at the stove, grating potatoes and slipping them into broth to make* klubb. *You can serve these dumplings with New England boiled dinner, corned beef, or pot roast. This also is good with* ribbe *(loin rib of pork). One of our family favorites was* klubb *alongside smoked pork butt and cabbage, served with mustard and* flatbrød.

> 12 russet or Yukon Gold potatoes
> Flour (half white and half barley, oat, or rye)
> 1 teaspoon fresh or dried thyme
> ½ teaspoon salt
> Salt pork or fresh pork, such as ham,
>     thick bacon, or tenderloin pork roast,
>     chopped into 1-inch pieces (optional)
> Stock or soup for simmering

Grate as many raw, peeled potatoes as are needed (12 potatoes will serve 6 to 8 people). Do not drain the potato liquid that accumulates. Add enough flour mixture, a little at a time, to make a dough of the same consistency as meatballs. Add thyme and salt.

Dip your hands in water before forming each dumpling. Dumplings should be about the size of medium-sized meatballs. Inside of each dumpling, press a piece of salt pork or fresh pork.

Drop the dumplings into boiling soup or stock and let simmer for 1 hour. Serve on a large heated platter.

# *Blodklubb* (Blood Potato Dumplings)

*Gudrun sometimes made this dish when Tante Borghild came to visit. Serves 8.*

6 to 8 potatoes, grated
1 pint cow or pig blood (usually
      available at a butcher or your
      grocery's meat counter)
3¼ cups rye flour
¾ cup water
1 tablespoon salt
1 teaspoon pepper
1 teaspoon ground cloves
1 teaspoon ground ginger
1½ cups suet, chopped
Melted butter and sugar or maple syrup

Bring a large pot of salted water to a boil. Combine grated potatoes, blood, flour, water, salt, pepper, cloves, and ginger in a large bowl and mix well. Form into large, flat dumplings. Inside each dumpling, place a lump of suet the size of a sugar cube. Simmer over medium-high heat for 30 minutes or until done (dumplings will hold together and feel solid). Drain and serve warm with a little melted butter and sugar, or brown dumplings in butter and serve with syrup.

## *Latkes*

*Sour cream and homemade applesauce make tasty accompaniments.*

> 2 eggs
> 2 cups grated raw potatoes, drained
> 1 small onion, grated
> 1 heaping tablespoon flour
> ½–1 teaspoon salt, to taste
> ¼ teaspoon baking powder
> Pinch of pepper
> Butter for frying

Beat eggs lightly. Add remaining ingredients to eggs and combine well. Drop mixture by tablespoonful into a hot, well-greased frying pan. Fry on both sides until golden brown. Serve immediately.

# Stuffed Cabbage Rolls

1¼ pounds lean ground beef,
    such as ground round
1 onion, chopped
1 egg
2 teaspoons salt
½ teaspoon pepper
½ teaspoon thyme
1 cup cooked brown rice
12 large cabbage leaves
Butter or oil for browning

**Sauce**
2 cans (8 ounces each) tomato sauce
¼ cup water
1 tablespoon brown sugar
1 tablespoon vinegar or lemon juice

Brown ground beef in a buttered frying pan with onion, egg, salt, pepper, and thyme, mixing well. Combine cooked brown rice with ground beef mixture. Set aside.

Bring a large pot of water to a boil and submerge cabbage leaves. Turn off heat and let stand for 5 minutes. (The cabbage leaves should be flexible enough to roll.) Drain. Place equal portions of meat mixture in center of each cabbage leaf. Roll up and fasten with a toothpick or string. Brown cabbage rolls in butter or oil in a skillet and transfer them to a serving dish.

While cabbage rolls are browning, heat tomato sauce and add water, brown sugar, and vinegar or lemon juice. Pour sauce over cabbage rolls and serve.

To make ahead, place browned cabbage rolls in a baking dish and make the sauce. When ready to serve, pour sauce over rolls and heat in a 350-degree oven for 30 minutes.

# *Surkål* (Sweet and Sour Cabbage)

*To this day, for our extended family, Thanksgiving and Christmas dinners are not complete without surkål. Use red cabbage in this dish for the holidays. This recipe serves 8 as a side, but you can easily double it, as it makes excellent leftovers and freezes well for up to three months.*

1 head red or green cabbage,
    chopped fine
1 cup water
1 cup sugar
½ cup vinegar
2 tablespoons caraway seeds
1½ tablespoons flour
1 tablespoon butter, softened

In a large saucepan, combine cabbage, water, sugar, vinegar, and caraway seeds and bring to a simmer. Let cook until cabbage is tender, about 20 minutes.

In a small bowl, blend flour with just enough water to make a paste. Add to cabbage mixture and stir for 5 to 10 minutes to heat through and thicken. Add butter to the top, let it melt, and stir it in to give the *surkål* a nice glaze.

# Soups and Stews

## ☙ Fruit and Vegetable Soups

Holiday Fruit Soup

Scandinavian Fruit Soup

Leek and Corn Soup

Pea Soup

Split Pea Soup

## ☙ Soups and Stews with Meat

Chicken Curry Stew

Chili con Carne

*Lapskaus* (Norwegian Beef Stew)

*Lapskaus* with Herbs

*Lapskaus* with Beef, Pork, and Ham

Sausage Lentil Soup

## FRUIT AND VEGETABLE SOUPS

# Holiday Fruit Soup

*Christmas dinner always began with a fruit soup like this one, which is still a favorite of ours. We also enjoyed it as the start of a meal at New Year's, as an evening snack served with rye bread, or as dessert with vanilla ice cream or whipped cream on top. It's best heated before serving—just warm, not hot. Be sure to allow time for the dried fruit to soak overnight. Serves 8.*

1 cup dried pitted prunes
½ cup raisins
½ cup dried apricots or dried peaches
1½ quarts water
¼ cup minute tapioca
1 cup sliced fresh apples or 1 cup sliced
    dried apples or pears
1 can (14.5 ounces) red sour
    cherries, drained
½ cup grape juice
½ cup orange juice
½ cup sugar
1 tablespoon grated orange peel

Soak prunes, raisins, and apricots or peaches in 1½ quarts of water overnight in a 2½-quart saucepan.

The next day, cover the pan of water and dried fruit and simmer over very low heat for about 1 hour or until fruit is tender. Add tapioca and cook until tapioca is almost clear, about 10 minutes. Stir in apples, cherries, grape juice, orange juice, sugar, and orange peel. Continue to cook over low heat until tapioca is fully clear, about 10 minutes more. Pour into a serving bowl set over a candle warmer.

# Scandinavian Fruit Soup

*This is a lighter, spicier version of fruit soup, made with fresh fruit and no tapioca.*
*Makes 6 to 8 servings.*

    1 orange, peeled and sliced
    1 lemon, thinly sliced
    2 cups water
    ¼ cup lemon juice
    6 whole cloves
    1 stick cinnamon
    3 Bosc, Anjou, or Comice pears,
        cored and sliced
    3 golden delicious apples, cored and sliced
    2 packages (12 ounces each) frozen dark
        sweet cherries, thawed and drained
    ½ cup sugar
    2 tablespoons cornstarch

Combine orange and lemon slices with water, lemon juice, cloves, and cinnamon. Bring to a boil and cook over low heat for 15 minutes. Remove cinnamon and cloves. Add pears, apples, cherries, and sugar to liquid. Blend cornstarch with a little water and add to fruit. Cook, stirring gently, until thick and clear, about 10 minutes.

# Leek and Corn Soup

*The red bell peppers make this soup a pretty salmon color.*

1 tablespoon olive oil
2 cloves garlic, minced
1 large leek, washed well and chopped
1 red bell pepper, chopped
2 bay leaves
6 cups corn kernels (fresh or frozen
    shoepeg corn), divided
4 cups chicken broth
1 teaspoon dried basil
1 teaspoon kosher salt
¼ teaspoon dried thyme
⅛ teaspoon freshly ground black pepper
Pinch of cayenne pepper
1 cup milk
1 tablespoon minced fresh parsley

Heat oil in a soup pot. Sauté the garlic and leek until the leek softens and turns golden. Stir in bell pepper, bay leaves, 5 cups of the corn, broth, basil, salt, thyme, and black and cayenne peppers. Bring to a boil, reduce to a simmer, cover, and cook for 20 minutes. Uncover, remove from heat, and let cool until the soup can be safely handled. Discard bay leaves. Puree soup in blender until smooth. Return soup to pot, add milk, parsley, and reserved cup of corn, and heat gently.

# Pea Soup

*We eat this soup not only in the cold of winter but all year round. It freezes well, and sometimes I freeze it in serving-size portions. Eddie always pureed this soup in the blender after cooking, but I serve it as is. I often wait to add the carrots and onion until the soup is about 30 minutes from being done, which makes them tender but still distinct. You can reduce the peppercorns and red pepper if you like a mild soup. This recipe serves about 8 people a meal-size portion.  —Irene*

> 2 packages (8 ounces each) dried
>     green split peas
> 3 large onions, diced
> 1 stalk celery, diced
> 3 quarts cold water
> 1 tablespoon peppercorns
> Cayenne pepper or dried
>     red pepper (optional)
> Ham bone (optional)
> 4 large carrots, diced (about 2 cups)
> Chopped parsley, dried red pepper, or
>     nutmeg for garnish

Slowly simmer dried peas, onions, and celery in 3 quarts of water for 2 hours. Add peppercorns, a sprinkle of cayenne or dried red pepper, and ham bone, if using. Simmer gently for another hour to deepen the flavors, adding the diced carrots about 30 minutes before serving. Add water if the broth thickens too much. Garnish with chopped parsley, dried red pepper, or nutmeg.

# Split Pea Soup

*When we have ham and I know I'm going to make this soup later, I put the bone in the freezer until I'm ready to make it. If the ham bone has significant meat on it, I reduce the amount of salt to 1 teaspoon. Gudrun used a full tablespoon of black pepper, but you may wish to use as little as a teaspoon. This recipe doubles well and can be pureed before serving if you like. Eddie always pureed his, but I usually serve it right from the big pot I cooked it in without blending. I like this soup with rye bread and thinly sliced cheese.  —Irene*

1 package (20 ounces) yellow or
   green split peas
12 cups water
1 medium onion, diced fine
4 tablespoons (½ stick) butter
1–2 teaspoons salt
1 teaspoon–1 tablespoon pepper, to taste
1 ham bone
4 carrots, peeled and diced
Croutons, dried red pepper, sliced scallions,
   or lemon wedges for garnish

Rinse and drain the dried split peas in several changes of water, picking them over carefully for any stones. In a large, heavy kettle, combine the dried split peas with the water, onion, butter, salt, and pepper. Add the ham bone, cover the pot, and bring to a boil. Boil rapidly for about 30 minutes. Lower the heat and let soup simmer for 1 to 1½ hours, or until the dried peas are very tender. Add the diced carrots and simmer about 30 minutes longer.

Remove the ham bone; slice any meat that is on the bone and put it in the soup. Serve the soup piping hot. Garnish with croutons, a sprinkle of red pepper, sliced scallions, a squeeze of lemon, or any combination thereof.

## SOUPS AND STEWS WITH MEAT

# Chicken Curry Stew

*If desired, accompany with brown, basmati, or jasmine rice and a green vegetable.*
*Serves 4 generously. This makes very good leftovers, as the flavors settle in.*

½ cup flour
2 teaspoons salt
⅛ teaspoon pepper
2½- to 3-pound broiler-fryer
    chicken, cut up
4 tablespoons (½ stick) butter
1 medium onion, chopped
2 tablespoons chopped parsley
1 garlic clove, crushed
1 can (32 ounces) tomatoes, with juice
2–3 teaspoons Jamaican curry
    powder, to taste
1 teaspoon coriander
½ teaspoon thyme
¼ cup raisins

Combine flour, salt, and pepper and dredge chicken pieces in the flour mixture. In
a heavy frying pan, heat butter over medium heat and brown chicken pieces. Add
onion, parsley, and garlic to chicken and stir to combine. Add tomatoes, curry powder,
coriander, and thyme. Cover and simmer about 45 minutes. Add raisins. Simmer
10 minutes longer or until chicken is tender.

# Chili con Carne

*This is good served with raw carrots and celery, pineapple rings with cottage cheese, and flatbrød or toast. You may also use 2 cups of dried lentils, simmered until tender, instead of the ground beef, a substitution Gudrun made when she was seeking heart-healthy meals. Some other variations are to add 1 cup of grated zucchini and 1 cup of grated carrots instead of the meat. But the traditional Gudrun way is this version. Since this is spicy, we drink lots of ice cold milk with it.*

1 large onion, chopped fine
2 stalks of celery, chopped fine
1 tablespoon butter or oil
2 pounds ground round beef
1 teaspoon of salt
1–2 tablespoons chili powder
2 cans (10.5 ounces each) condensed tomato soup
2 cans (15 ounces each) kidney beans, drained
   (optional: use double the amount of kidney beans)
1 can (32 ounces) stewed tomatoes (optional)
1 can (15 ounces) tiny white Italian beans (cannellini), drained

In a large pot, brown onion and celery in butter or oil. Add the meat and brown it. Add salt and 1 tablespoon of the chili powder. Add tomato soup, kidney beans, stewed tomatoes if using, and cannellini beans. If desired, add more chili powder to taste. (Our family likes it spicy.) Let simmer over low heat for 1 hour.

# *Lapskaus* (Norwegian Beef Stew)

*Whenever my mother would cook* lapskaus *(and there are many ways to make it), my dad would exclaim that no one could make* lapskaus *like his sister Anna in Norway could. He longed to have that taste again.*

*Lapskaus can be made with fresh or leftover meat and potatoes. It can be like a stew or a hash. My dad liked it with a lot of gravy. (Indeed, sometimes I think his favorite part of the meal was a second helping of gravy, into which he'd break up flatbrød. He ate that mixture as if it was his dessert!) The last time I made* lapskaus, *our cousin Pål was with us, and he said no, this was not the real* lapskaus—*the real* lapskaus *has every ingredient chopped in teeny, tiny pieces. I guess everyone has his or her own favorite* lapskaus. *—Irene*

¼ cup butter or canola oil

2 pounds of boneless beef, diced in
  ¼-inch or smaller cubes

2 medium onions, diced

2 cups water

1½ teaspoons salt

½ teaspoon pepper

½ teaspoon ginger

½ teaspoon sugar

Juice of ½ lemon

6 medium potatoes, peeled and diced
  into 1-inch pieces

4 carrots, peeled and diced into 1-inch pieces

Heat butter or oil in a large pan, add the meat, and brown well on all sides. Add the onions, water, salt, pepper, ginger, sugar, and lemon juice. Cover and bring to a boil. Lower the heat and cook at least 30 minutes or until the meat is very tender, up to 1½ hours. You can cook the meat longer, adding water as needed, so the meat is very tender. Add the potatoes and carrots and cook until vegetables are tender, about 20 minutes longer.

## *Lapskaus* with Herbs

*This recipe serves 8 to 10 people and is good with a lot of spices to taste. You can make this stew with leftover beef and potatoes cut into small pieces as for hash, covered with water, and cooked for 30 minutes before adding vegetables. It is best made the day before.*

2 pounds beef (chuck or round steak), cubed
Shortening
1½ cups sliced onion
Boiling water
1 teaspoon dried basil
1 teaspoon salt or to taste
Pepper to taste (Gudrun used
    whole peppercorns)
1 bay leaf
½ teaspoon dried thyme
½ teaspoon celery salt or to taste
2 cups diced carrots
4 cups finely diced raw potatoes
Sprigs of fresh parsley
Water, chicken or beef broth, or
    1 bouillon cube, as needed

Brown cubed meat in the shortening. Add onion. Add boiling water to cover meat. Reduce the heat and simmer until tender. (This may take up to 2 hours.) After about an hour, add basil, salt, pepper, bay leaf, thyme, and celery salt. Add carrots and simmer for 10 minutes, then add the potatoes. Add parsley. Add water, chicken or beef broth, or a bouillon cube as needed to have enough gravy. The mixture should cook down so that no thickening is needed, but watch it carefully so that it does not burn or stick to the bottom. Keep stirring occasionally, and add more liquid to keep the mixture moist and to make lots of gravy.

# *Lapskaus* with Beef, Pork, and Ham

*For variety, garnish this stew with finely chopped fresh cilantro. You can also add one or two cubes of beef or vegetable bouillon and reduce the salt. Serve with cooked carrots, cucumber salad, beet salad, and dark bread like rye to soak up the gravy. Serves 4 to 6 people.*

> 3½ cups water
> 1½ pounds stewing beef, such as round
>    roast or chuck, cubed into tiny pieces
> ½ pound of pork, diced
> ¼ pound of salt pork or ham (optional)
> 2 onions, diced
> 3 bay leaves
> 6 whole peppercorns
> 6 medium potatoes, peeled and diced
> 2 teaspoons salt
> 3 tablespoons chopped fresh parsley or cilantro

In a large pot, bring the water to a boil. Add the beef, pork, and salt pork and boil, uncovered, for 4 to 5 minutes. There should be enough water in the pot to cover the meat; add more if necessary. Reduce heat to low, skim foam from the surface, and add the onions, bay leaves, and peppercorns. Cover and simmer about 45 minutes to 1 hour. Add the potatoes and simmer another hour, until the potatoes are soft and begin to dissolve. Add the salt and stir. Discard the bay leaves. Sprinkle with chopped parsley or cilantro to garnish.

# Sausage Lentil Soup

*This soup can be varied in a number of ways. It is excellent without the bacon and sausage, and you can add vegetarian bacon bits if desired for flavor. You can also omit the salt and substitute garlic powder or a crushed garlic clove. Try adding fresh spinach and garnishing the soup with chopped fresh parsley or cilantro. You may also reduce the bacon to 2 slices and omit the sausage, then stir in 6 frankfurters, thinly sliced, and 1 teaspoon steak sauce just before serving. This soup serves 8 as a side with dinner, or 4 as a main dish.*

1 pound dried lentils

8 cups water

2 cans (14 ounces each) whole, stewed,
  or diced tomatoes, with juice

2 bay leaves

1 teaspoon salt

1 teaspoon pepper

8 slices bacon, diced

1 cup diced or thinly sliced carrots

1 cup chopped celery

1 medium onion, diced

2 pounds ground pork sausage, browned and diced

Wash lentils and combine with water, tomatoes, bay leaves, salt, and pepper. Bring to a boil and reduce heat. In another pan, fry bacon until limp, then add carrots, celery, and onions and sauté over medium heat for 15 minutes, stirring constantly. Drain off fat and add bacon mixture and browned sausage to lentils. Simmer 1 hour on top of stove, or cook 4 to 6 hours in a slow cooker set on high.

# Meat Entrees

Marinade

## ✿ Beef

Barbecue Beef

Chop Suey

Burgundy Beef Ragout

Chinese Beef and Tomatoes

Coffee Round Steak

Easy Oven Stew

Gudrun's Good Hamburger

Ground Beef and Eggs

Norwegian Meatballs

Pot Roast

Sweet and Sour Pot Roast

Stew Meat over Noodles

## ✿ Lamb

*Far I Kal* (Lamb and Cabbage)

Lamb Roast

## ✿ Pork

Pork Chops with Colored Cinnamon Apples

Ham Dinner

## ✿ Poultry

Gudrun's Famous Chicken and Gravy

Chicken and Ham Veronique

Chicken Fricassee

Chicken D'Pollis

Fried Chicken with Gravy

Wild Rice Chicken Supreme

# Marinade

*This marinade can be used on any meat for barbecue.*

1½ cups vegetable oil
¾ cup soy sauce
½ cup wine vinegar
⅓ cup lemon juice
¼ cup Worcestershire sauce
2 tablespoons dry mustard
1 tablespoon coarse ground pepper
2¼ teaspoons salt
1½ teaspoons dried parsley flakes
2 cloves garlic, crushed

Combine all ingredients and mix well. Use right away or store for 1 week in the refrigerator or a few months in the freezer.

# BEEF

## Barbecue Beef

*Serves 12 generously.*

> 4 pounds hamburger
> 1 onion, chopped
> 1 green pepper, chopped
> ¼ teaspoon salt
> ¼ teaspoon pepper
> 2 cans (10.5 ounces each) condensed tomato soup
> 2 cans (10.5 ounces each) condensed cream of mushroom soup
> 12 hamburger buns

Brown meat, onion, and green pepper in a buttered frying pan. Add salt and pepper. Mix together in a pot with tomato and mushroom soups until warm. Serve on hamburger buns.

# Chop Suey

*Gudrun used a can of chop suey vegetables, but this recipe calls for a variety of fresh or canned vegetables instead. Allow 1 hour for the meat to chill before cutting. Serves 4.*

1 pound flank steak, round steak, veal, or center-cut pork chops

Soy sauce to taste

2-inch piece of ginger, peeled and minced

3 cloves garlic, minced

1 tablespoon plus 2 teaspoons sugar, divided

2 tablespoons olive oil or corn oil, divided

1 cup chopped celery

½ cup chopped onions

1 package (8 ounces) fresh bean sprouts or 1 can (16 ounces) bamboo shoots, drained

½ pound snow peas or 1 can (5 ounces) sliced canned water chestnuts, drained

½ pound bok choy or Chinese cabbage, cut in 1-inch pieces

2 tablespoons molasses

1 teaspoon salt

Dried chop suey noodles

Chopped green onions

Cooked rice

Place the meat in the freezer for at least 1 hour before cutting it. Using a sharp knife, slice the meat across the grain into very thin slices, about ⅛ inch wide and ½ inch to 1 inch long. Toss the meat with soy sauce, minced ginger, minced garlic, and 2 teaspoons sugar and marinate at least 30 minutes.

In a wok or large frying pan, heat 1 tablespoon of oil over medium-high heat, add vegetables, and stir fry briefly, 1 to 3 minutes. Remove vegetables from the pan and set aside. Add 1 tablespoon of oil to the pan, raise heat to high, and add the sliced marinated meat. Stir and quickly cook until just done.

Lower heat to medium-high and return vegetables to the pan. Add molasses, remaining 1 tablespoon sugar, and salt and stir to combine and heat through. Sprinkle with chop suey noodles and chopped green onions and serve over rice.

# Burgundy Beef Ragout

*This serves 6 to 8 people. Be sure to allow time for marinating and simmering.*

> 2 tablespoons red wine or ⅛ cup soy sauce
> 1 teaspoon sugar
> 2 pounds stew meat (beef or game), cut into 1-inch pieces
> 2 tablespoons butter
> 2 tablespoons Beau Monde seasoning salt
> 1 can (15 ounces) tomato sauce
> ½ cup burgundy or other red wine
> 1 teaspoon thyme
> ½ bay leaf
> 1 can (4 ounces) whole button mushrooms, liquid reserved,
>     or 4 ounces fresh mushrooms
> 1 cup sliced carrots
> Buttered noodles or cooked brown rice

Mix wine or soy sauce and sugar to make a marinade. Marinate the cubed meat mixture in the refrigerator for at least 30 minutes.

Brown meat in butter in a large, heavy saucepan. Sprinkle with Beau Monde during browning. Add tomato sauce, wine, thyme, bay leaf, and liquid from drained mushrooms. Cover and simmer for 2½ hours. Add mushrooms and carrots. Simmer covered 30 to 40 minutes more until carrots are tender. Serve over buttered noodles or brown rice.

# Chinese Beef and Tomatoes

*Serves 4 generously.*

> 1½ pounds round steak, partially frozen
> ¾ cup soy sauce
> 1 teaspoon sugar
> ¼ cup vegetable oil
> 1 clove garlic
> ¾ teaspoon ginger
> 2 green, red, or yellow bell peppers, seeded and julienned
> 3 large tomatoes, peeled and cut in eighths
> 2 teaspoons cornstarch mixed with 2 tablespoons soy sauce
> Cooked rice

Cut steak across the grain in paper-thin slices and place in a large bowl. Combine soy sauce and sugar in a small bowl and pour over meat. Let marinate in the refrigerator for 30 minutes, turning meat after 15 minutes. Heat vegetable oil in large skillet and add garlic and ginger. Cook for 1 to 2 minutes. Add peppers and sauté, stirring, for 3 minutes. Add beef and marinade liquid and cook another 3 minutes. Add tomatoes. Cover and simmer another couple of minutes. Gently stir cornstarch mixed with soy sauce into the mixture and cook 1 minute more. Serve with rice.

# Coffee Round Steak

*We like to serve this dish with mashed or steamed potatoes and fresh steamed peas or green beens. Cooked carrots are a good addition, too. This recipe makes a lot of gravy and serves 6.*

Vegetable oil
2 pounds round steak (beef or game),
    sliced into narrow strips
2 cups sliced onions
1½ cups strong coffee
1 cup red wine
¼ cup flour
1 can (4 ounces) mushroom stems and pieces, drained,
    or 4 ounces fresh mushrooms, sliced
1 tablespoon horseradish
¼ teaspoon garlic powder
Pinch of salt
Pinch of pepper

Heat oil in a large skillet. Add beef and brown meat in hot oil. Add onions and sauté until tender. Add remaining ingredients and mix well; cover and simmer on low heat for 1½ hours.

# Easy Oven Stew

*Serve this with a tossed spinach salad and good whole-grain or French bread. Serves 6.*

¼ cup flour
2 teaspoons seasoning salt
¼ teaspoon ground pepper
¼ teaspoon paprika
2 pounds beef stew meat
2 tablespoons safflower oil
4 onions, quartered
4 carrots cut into 1-inch pieces
1 cup celery cut into 1-inch pieces
1 can (18 ounces) tomato sauce
1 cup water

Preheat oven to 400 degrees. Combine flour, salt, pepper, and paprika in a paper bag. Divide beef into two portions and drop into the bag one portion at a time. Shake until coated. Mix coated beef with oil in 3-quart casserole. Bake uncovered for 30 minutes. Stir once and add vegetables, tomato sauce, and water. Mix well. Lower heat to 350 degrees, cover the casserole, and bake for 45 minutes or until meat and vegetables are fork tender.

# Gudrun's Good Hamburger

*Serve these hamburgers with boiled vegetables, steamed or mashed potatoes, and salad.*
*Or try serving them open-faced on toasted rye bread. Serves 3 to 4.*

> 1 pound ground round steak
> 1 small onion, grated fine (juice and pulp)
> 2 tablespoons heavy cream or
>     undiluted evaporated milk
> 1 teaspoon red wine vinegar
> ¾ teaspoon Worcestershire sauce
> ¼ teaspoon pepper
> ¼ teaspoon crushed thyme
> 1 tablespoon butter
> Pinch of nutmeg

In a large bowl, mix all ingredients except butter and nutmeg and form mixture into patties. Brown patties in butter and sprinkle with nutmeg. Serve with drippings in pan.

# Ground Beef and Eggs

*Serve with cooked vegetables, beets, and salad. Serves 6.*

> 2 pounds lean ground beef
> 1 onion, diced
> Dash of salt and pepper
> Dash of seasoning salt
> 1 egg per person

In a large frying pan, brown meat with onion and seasonings. Add water to barely cover ground beef and let simmer until meat is cooked through. Break one egg for each person on top of meat. Cover and let egg poach until done.

# Norwegian Meatballs

*Meatballs were a cornerstone of Gudrun's menu, usually served with mashed or steamed new potatoes, peas or beans, cranberry sauce or tytebaer (lingonberry) sauce, flatbrød, raw carrots and celery, pickled cucumber salad, and carrot salad. They were also a favorite of her grandsons. On many a Sunday, Erik and Quinn would engage in an all-out grudge match to see who could eat the most meatballs. On one occasion, the boys' friend Richard Peddie joined them for lunch. Richard loved the meatballs so much that he threw all his manners out the window, picked up his plate, and licked it clean. Gudrun delighted in the boy's unbridled appreciation for good food and ever after kept a special place in her heart for Richard Peddie.*

*Gudrun would ask the butcher to grind the meat five or six times to get the best texture. (You can chop your own meat using the cutting blade in the food processor.) This recipe serves 6 to 8 people with ample sides. The meatballs can be frozen, and they are delicious as leftovers. A small ice-cream scoop makes it easy to form consistent-sized meatballs.*

1 cup whole milk

1 bouillon cube

1½ pounds beef chuck, ¼ pound veal, and
    ¼ pound pork (have butcher grind
    all meats together, very fine)

1 tablespoon onion, chopped fine

1 egg

1 teaspoon nutmeg

1 teaspoon salt

½ teaspoon pepper

Dash of ginger, mace, marjoram, and allspice

Suet or other fat to grease the pan

2 whole bell peppers, chopped celery, or whole carrot

2 whole black peppercorns

1 teaspoon flour dissolved in 1 tablespoon
    cold water, or more as needed for gravy consistency

In a saucepan, heat milk with bouillon cube. Meanwhile, in a large bowl, combine meat with onion. In a separate bowl, lightly blend egg and spices with a fork. Add egg mixture to meat and onion and mix thoroughly with hands. Add a little milk at a time and beat until mixed thoroughly. Form mixture into 1-inch meatballs.

Heat suet or other fat in a heavy frying pan. Brown meatballs. Add whole bell peppers, chopped celery, or whole carrot, peppercorns, and enough water to cover generously. Simmer until meatballs are cooked through. Discard vegetables before serving. Whisk flour-water mixture into meatball liquid to make gravy. If the meatball cooking liquid gets very low or cooks off, add more water. Continue to simmer until gravy is thickened. (You may need to add more flour-water paste to thicken the gravy to your liking.)

# Pot Roast

*Gudrun's pot roast is especially good in cold weather. She added a lot of pepper for Irving, who loved pepper. And what he loved best was the rich gravy: when he finished everything else, he would take another helping of gravy, crumble flatbrød into it, and eat it up. This hearty recipe yields 9 to 12 servings, about ⅓ pound of meat per person. Serve with steamed or mashed potatoes, or with the potatoes cooked with the roast.*

> 3–4 pounds chuck roast
> Pinch of ground ginger
> Pinch of salt
> Pinch of pepper
> 1 cup onions, sliced or diced
> 4 or 5 whole peppercorns
> 3 bay leaves
> Pinch of allspice
> ½ cup boiling water or
>     hot vegetable broth
> 2 celery stalks, chopped
> 2 carrots, chopped
> 2 whole potatoes, peeled
> 1 bouillon cube

Bring roast to room temperature. Preheat oven to 325 degrees. Trim fat from roast and set aside. Sprinkle meat with ginger, salt, and pepper. Heat fat trimmings in a frying pan, then add the onions and roast. Brown roast on each side. Add peppercorns, bay leaves, and allspice. Add boiling water or vegetable broth. Add celery and carrots. Bake for 50 minutes, then baste and reduce heat to 300 degrees. Add potatoes and bouillon cube. Bake for 2 hours more.

# Sweet and Sour Pot Roast

*Serves 12 people, allowing ⅓ pound of meat per person. This is delicious the next day. Serve with mashed potatoes or rice.*

4 pounds pot roast
Flour mixed with salt and pepper
Butter or oil for browning meat
    (or use extra fat cut off from roast)
1 cup stock or bouillon from a cube
¼ cup honey
Juice of 2 lemons
3 stalks celery, chopped
3 carrots, chopped
2 onions, sliced
12 peppercorns
1 garlic clove, minced
1 bay leaf

Dredge meat in seasoned flour. In a large heavy pot with a cover, brown the meat slowly in butter or fat for 20 minutes. Add all remaining ingredients and simmer, covered, for 3½ hours, adding more liquid if it cooks off.

# Stew Meat over Noodles

*Serve this with green vegetables, cranberry sauce, flatbrød, and salad. Serves 4 to 6.*

4 tablespoons (½ stick) butter, divided
1½ pounds stew meat (beef, elk, or antelope),
    cut in 2-inch cubes
1 package powdered onion soup mix
3 cups water, divided
1 can (8 ounces) mushroom stems and
    pieces, drained, or 8 ounces fresh
    sliced mushrooms
5 small carrots, grated
1 pound medium egg noodles

In a large pot, heat 2 tablespoons butter and brown the meat in it. Add soup mix and 2 cups water. Cover and simmer for 30 minutes. Add remaining 1 cup water. Cover and simmer another 30 minutes. Add mushrooms and carrots. Cover and simmer another 30 minutes.

Meanwhile, cook and drain noodles, then toss with remaining 2 tablespoons butter. Serve beef over noodles.

# LAMB

## *Far I Kal* (Lamb and Cabbage)

*This dish serves 6 and can easily be doubled. It also freezes well. Serve with mashed or steamed potatoes.*

> 1½ pounds shoulder or breast of lamb
> 2 tablespoons vegetable oil
> 3 cups water
> 1 head of cabbage (2 pounds)
> 3 tablespoons flour
> 1½ teaspoons salt
> 1½ teaspoons peppercorns

Wipe lamb with a clean, damp cloth, trim off fat, and cut meat into 1-inch cubes or smaller. Heat the oil in a large saucepan with a tight-fitting cover; add the meat and brown on all sides. Add water and cook over medium heat for 20 to 30 minutes or until lamb is tender. Remove and discard outer leaves from the head of the cabbage; rinse cabbage and cut into 1-inch pieces. Discard the core of the cabbage. When the meat is tender, drain and reserve the liquid.

Place half the chopped cabbage in the saucepan. In a small bowl, blend flour, salt, and peppercorns. Sprinkle half the flour mixture over the cabbage. Layer meat over the cabbage and flour, add remaining cabbage, and sprinkle remaining flour mixture over the top. Pour 2⅓ cups of the reserved cooking liquid over the cabbage and lamb. Cover and cook over low heat for 1½ hours or until meat and cabbage are very tender. Serve immediately, while very hot.

# Lamb Roast

*This roast is delicious for Easter dinner with fresh mint or mint jelly and lamb gravy, plus mashed or roasted potatoes, cooked sliced carrot sticks, and carrot salad. Serves 10 to 12.*

> 5-pound leg of lamb roast, boneless or bone-in
> About 10 cloves of garlic, minced and slivered, to taste
> Salt and pepper, garlic powder, and rosemary to
>     sprinkle over lamb, to taste
> 1 prune
> 1 onion, sliced or whole
> 2 cups milk or half-and-half, heated slightly
> 1 cube chicken bouillon or Kitchen Bouquet (optional)

Preheat oven to 375 degrees. Wipe roast clean and rub with minced garlic. Cut slits on surface of roast and insert a sliver of fresh garlic into each slit. Combine salt, pepper, garlic powder, and rosemary and sprinkle all over the lamb before placing it into a roasting pan. Add the prune and sliced or whole onion to the pan and place lamb in oven for 15 minutes.

Turn over roast using spoons (do not poke with a fork), then lower heat to 300 degrees and return lamb to oven. Bake for 2 hours or until meat thermometer inserted into the center registers 145 degrees for medium rare. Remove and discard the onion and prune. Remove the lamb from the pan and place on the carving board to rest for 15 minutes before cutting.

While the lamb rests, make the gravy. Place roasting pan on top of stove and add about 2 cups of milk or half-and-half to the drippings. Bring to a simmer over medium heat, stirring constantly with a wooden Norwegian sauce stirrer or wire whisk. Simmer and stir until gravy thickens. You may choose to add a chicken bouillon cube or a little Kitchen Bouquet for color.

# PORK

## Pork Chops with Colored Cinnamon Apples

*Serve with scalloped or mashed potatoes and a cooked green vegetable such as green beans, broccoli, asparagus, or Brussels sprouts. We like to serve this with applesauce in addition to the colored cinnamon apple slices. Serves 2 to 4 people, allowing one thick or two thin pork chops per person.*

4 pork chops, some fat trimmed and reserved
Pinch of apple pie spice
Pinch of salt and pepper
Vegetable or potato cooking water
½ cup chopped onion
1 bouillon cube
Boiling water

**Colored Cinnamon Apples**
2 apples, cored and sliced
½ cup water
½ cup sugar
1 lemon slice
1 teaspoon lemon juice
1 teaspoon cinnamon heart candies

Sprinkle pork chops with apple pie spice, salt, and pepper and let sit. Render the reserved pork fat in a frying pan, then place chops in pan to brown. Add vegetable or potato cooking water, just a little here and there to keep chops moist. When chops are almost cooked through, add onion, bouillon cube, and a little boiling water to make a light gravy.

While the chops are cooking, prepare the apples. Place sliced apples in another frying pan and add water, sugar, lemon slice, lemon juice, and cinnamon candies. Simmer until apples are soft and candies have melted to flavor and color the apple rings, and serve with pork chops.

# Ham Dinner

*Serve this dish with apricot sauce gravy, baked sweet potatoes, creamed potatoes or scalloped potatoes, green beans, and individual servings of pineapple rings with cottage cheese in the center, served on a lettuce leaf. Corn casserole, fresh corn, or cream cabbage also make tasty accompaniments.*

> 5–10 pound ham, with or without bone
> Whole cloves
> Brown sugar
> 1 teaspoon dry mustard
> 3 to 4 cups apricot nectar, heated
> 1 teaspoon vinegar (optional)
> 1 tablespoon of all-purpose or potato flour
>     dissolved in 1–2 tablespoons water

Preheat oven to 325 degrees. Score the ham all over and stud with whole cloves. Sprinkle with brown sugar and dry mustard. Bake for 20 minutes per pound, basting with the heated apricot nectar every 10 minutes. When finished, spoon off ham drippings for gravy and pour vinegar, if using, over the ham.

To make the gravy, heat ham drippings in a small saucepan over medium heat. If there is not enough liquid, add another cup of apricot nectar and ½ cup brown sugar. Stir in flour-water mixture and continue stirring while simmering until mixture has thickened.

## POULTRY

# Gudrun's Famous Chicken and Gravy

*I don't know if it was because the chicken was freshly killed and plucked that day, the fresh creamery butter she used, or the constant basting she did while it was cooking both on top of the stove and in the oven, but my mother's chicken was delicious. We raised and killed our own chickens. There was a tree stump in the back of the barn and someone would hold the chicken down on the stump so that its neck was flat. Then my dad would come down with the ax, and off came the head. The chicken would run around in circles without its head, blood flying out all over. When the chicken had died, my dad would hold it by its legs and dip it in boiling water. We would then lay it on the table and pull off all the feathers. Then my mother would cut the chicken in quarters, so that each piece had some white and some dark meat. That's when she started cooking. She served this dish with mashed potatoes swimming in gravy, homemade cranberry sauce or tytebaer (lingonberry) sauce, flatbrød, green beans, salad, pineapple slices and cottage cheese, and always with her carrot salad. She made cole slaw and potato salad to accompany the chicken for picnics. Gudrun usually served a one-quarter chicken portion per person. —Irene*

> 3 pounds chicken legs, breasts, and thighs
> Lemon juice
> Pancake mix (Gudrun used Aunt Jemima brand) or flour
> 1 teaspoon paprika
> 1 teaspoon salt or onion salt
> ½ teaspoon pepper
> Pinch of ginger
> Pinch of cardamom
> 4 tablespoons (½ stick) butter
> Vegetable oil
> 1 small onion
> ½ cup hot vegetable broth or boiling water for basting

**Gravy**

1 cup milk

1 teaspoon Kitchen Bouquet seasoning
    sauce or 1 bouillon cube (optional)

1 teaspoon flour (if needed)

Wash chicken pieces and soak in water with a little lemon juice for about 20 minutes. Drain chicken and pat dry with paper towel or dish towel. Place pancake mix, paprika, salt, pepper, ginger, and cardamom in a bag. Shake chicken in the bag, and let the chicken rest in the bag to take in flour, about 10 minutes.

Preheat oven to 325 degrees. Heat butter and a little oil in a frying pan and brown chicken over medium heat until golden brown on all sides. Place chicken pieces in one layer in a metal or glass pan (reserving drippings in frying pan). Peel the onion and, with the tip of a knife, scrape about a teaspoon of onion juice over each piece of chicken.

Pour drippings from the frying pan over chicken, cover with aluminum foil, and bake for 1½ to 2 hours until juices run clear, removing foil after the first hour. Baste with vegetable broth or water every 15 minutes for the remainder of baking time.

Remove chicken from the baking dish, keep the meat warm, and use the drippings to make the gravy. Heat milk in the top of a double boiler and stir in drippings from baking pan, stirring constantly. Add Kitchen Bouquet to enhance the color or bouillon cube, if using. Simmer gravy, stirring constantly, until thick. If gravy is too thin, whisk in 1 teaspoon flour at a time (or make additional thickener by combining small amounts of water and flour to make a paste, and whisk that in). Pour some gravy over the chicken before serving and serve the remainder in a gravy boat.

Note: If you have any leftovers, make a chicken pie: Preheat the oven to 325 degrees. Combine remaining gravy, boned chicken, vegetables, and potatoes and pour over a prepared crust in a pie plate. In a separate bowl, beat together an egg yolk, some nutmeg, and a little milk. Add chopped celery. Pour over chicken and other leftovers and top with a second crust. Bake for 40 minutes.

# Chicken and Ham Veronique

*Gudrun served this dish in puff pastry shells, which she called patty shells. Serves 4.*

2 tablespoons butter
½ cup sliced mushrooms
¼ cup chopped onion
1 small clove garlic, minced
1 cup cubed cooked chicken
½ cup ham cut in 2-inch strips
1 can (10.75 ounces) condensed cream of chicken soup
½ cup milk
½ cup green grapes, cut in half
8 puff pastry shells

In a medium saucepan, melt butter over medium heat. Add mushrooms, onion, and garlic and sauté for a few minutes, until onion is golden. Mix in chicken, ham, soup, milk, and grapes. Cook until heated through, stirring occasionally. Serve in pastry shells, two shells per person.

# Chicken Fricassee

*This is a good way to prepare older chickens, as they are always made tender by long and slow cooking. Gudrun often made this dish and served it on baking powder biscuits or with dumplings to the Lutheran Church Ladies Group, along with mint juleps with fresh sprigs of mint from the garden. Begin this recipe several hours or one day ahead.*

*We like to use the Norwegian birch sticks for stirring sauces so they won't get lumps or stick. These are always foolproof. If you don't have them, you can use a wire whisk to make the sauce smooth.*

3½ pounds chicken legs, thighs, and breasts,
    cut into pieces (or you can cook a whole hen
    chicken for 1½ hours with a piece of ginger
    and a whole onion in the cooking water)
Pinch of salt and pepper
1-inch piece of gingerroot, grated
1 whole onion
3 quarts boiling water
½ cup diced onion
½ cup diced celery
½ cup diced carrot

**Fricassee Sauce**
¼ cup poultry fat or butter
¼ cup flour
1½ cups hot chicken stock
½ cup hot cream
1 teaspoon salt
¼ teaspoon pepper

Place chicken in a large bowl and sprinkle with salt and pepper. Toss with grated ginger and add a whole onion, cover, and refrigerate for several hours or overnight.

Place chicken in a pot, add whole onion and ginger, cover with boiling water, and simmer over low heat, covered, for 3 hours. Add diced onion, celery, and carrot, and cook until vegetables are tender. Drain the chicken and vegetables and set aside. Discard the whole onion.

Let the chicken cool, remove the meat from the bone, and return the meat to the cream sauce before serving.

To make the sauce, melt fat or butter in a frying pan large enough to hold the chicken. Add flour, and, while stirring with a whisk, gradually pour in the hot chicken stock. Add the hot cream and continue stirring until gravy has thickened. Season gravy with salt and pepper and add chicken to pan, spooning gravy over chicken. Let cook a few more minutes and serve.

# Chicken D'Pollis

*This is excellent served with a side of pasta, polenta, or mashed potatoes.*

> 3 pounds chicken breasts, thighs, and legs
> 1 clove garlic
> 2 tablespoons oil or butter, divided
> ½ cup minced onion
> 2 cans (6 ounces each) tomato paste
> 1 can (15 ounces) tomato puree
> ½ cup water
> ½ cup chopped green olives
> ¼ cup sliced pimento-stuffed olives
> Several stalks of celery, chopped
> Chopped parsley to taste

Rinse chicken and pat dry. Rub a large skillet with garlic. Add 1 tablespoon oil or butter and place over medium heat. Cook chicken until golden brown. Remove chicken and set aside.

In the same skillet, add remaining 1 tablespoon butter or oil and cook minced onion until golden brown. Add tomato paste, tomato puree, water, green olives, stuffed olives, and celery. Simmer for 5 minutes. Return chicken to skillet and simmer, covered, over low heat at least 1 hour. You may need to add a little more water to prevent scorching the bottom of the pan and to keep the chicken moist and tender. A bit more water also makes a tasty sauce or gravy to serve with the chicken. Top with a sprinkle of chopped parsley.

# Fried Chicken with Gravy

*Serve with mashed potatoes, carrot salad or cole slaw, peas, and celery and carrot sticks.*

3½ pounds chicken pieces
Lemon juice or 1 teaspoon vinegar
Flour or pancake mix (Gudrun used Aunt Jemima brand)
Salt
Pepper
Paprika
2 tablespoons butter
1 onion

**Gravy**
Vegetable broth or water
1 to 1½ cups whole milk
1 teaspoon Kitchen Bouquet or 1 bouillon cube
1 teaspoon flour (if needed)

Preheat oven to 325 degrees. Wash chicken well in cold water and rub with a small amount of lemon juice diluted in water or with 1 teaspoon vinegar. Dry chicken with a paper towel.

Place a small amount of flour or pancake mix, salt, pepper, and paprika in a plastic bag. Shake chicken pieces in the flour mixture to coat. In a frying pan, heat butter over medium heat and brown the chicken pieces. Grate an onion over the pan, sprinkling onion and juice over the chicken pieces. Transfer chicken to an aluminum or glass baking dish. Cover with foil and bake until juices run clear, about 1½ hours, basting every 15 minutes. Remove foil for last ½ hour of baking.

When chicken is done, make the gravy. Remove chicken from pan and deglaze pan with a small amount of water or vegetable broth. In a separate pan, heat milk. Pour milk into deglazed pan and stir. If gravy is too light, add a chicken bouillon cube or Kitchen Bouquet. Let simmer until thick. You can add 1 teaspoon of flour if needed to thicken.

# Wild Rice Chicken Supreme

*Serves 6 to 8.*

1 box (16 ounces) long grain wild rice
⅓ cup chopped onion
⅓ cup butter
⅓ cup flour
1 teaspoon salt
Dash of ground black pepper
1 cup half-and-half
1 cup chicken broth
2 cups cooked cubed white meat chicken
⅓ cup chopped pimentos
⅓ cup chopped fresh parsley
3 tablespoons chopped blanched almonds

Preheat oven to 350 degrees and grease a 2-quart casserole. Cook wild rice according to directions on package. Meanwhile, sauté onion in butter. Blend in flour, salt, and pepper. Stir in half-and-half and chicken broth. Cook, stirring constantly, until thickened. Combine sauce with cooked rice, chicken, pimentos, parsley, and almonds. Pour mixture into casserole and bake until sauce is bubbly, about 45 minutes.

# Seafood Entrees

Boiled Codfish

Fillets Elegante

*Finnan Haddie* (Smoked Haddock)

*Fiskeboller* in Curried Cream Sauce

*Fiskeboller* in Cream Sauce with Sherry and Lobster

*Gravlaks*

*Gravlaks Saus* (Mustard Sauce for *Gravlaks*)

Hot Mustard Sauce

Gudrun's Fish

Eddie's Fish

Alaskan Halibut

*Lutefisk*

Shrimp Newburg

Tuna Potato Bake

# Boiled Codfish

*It is best not to cook the fish until your guests are seated, and then be ready to serve on a heated serving platter the moment it is done. You can use frozen fish for this recipe.*

Slice the codfish into four serving pieces, allowing about 8 ounces per person (for big fish eaters). Wrap fish in cheesecloth to keep it together. In a heavy stock pan that is about six inches deep or a greased fish-poaching pan, bring the water to a gentle boil. Gudrun always added ½ cup of salt for each quart of water, but you can use less if you prefer. She also added mustard seeds, coriander seeds, and whole black pepper to the water and let the water boil for about 10 or more minutes before gently adding the fish. Place fish slices in the gently boiling water and return to boil, then immediately reduce to a simmer. Simmer 5 to 8 minutes per pound of fish. As soon as the fish begins to slip from the bones, remove it from the water and serve instantly on the heated platter.

Gudrun served this with steamed or boiled new or russet potatoes, loads of melted butter, and steamed or boiled carrots and peas. Carrot salad is another good addition, and pickled cucumber salad is a must, as is *flatbrød* with butter. Serves 4.

# Fillets Elegante

*Serve with boiled or steamed new potatoes, peas and carrots, tossed salad, and* flatbrød.

1 pound frozen fish fillets, such
    as haddock or sole
2 tablespoons butter
1 teaspoon fresh ground pepper
1 can (10.75 ounces) condensed
    cream of shrimp soup
¼ cup grated Parmesan cheese
Dash of paprika
Lemon wedges

Preheat oven to 400 degrees and butter a baking dish. Thaw fillets in the refrigerator or under running cold water enough to separate them. Spread fillets with butter and arrange in the baking dish. Sprinkle with pepper. Pour soup over fillets and sprinkle with cheese and paprika. Bake for 25 minutes. Serve with lemon wedges.

## *Finnan Haddie* (Smoked Haddock)

*This recipe calls for soaking* finnan haddie *in cold water, but you could also do as Gudrun often did and simply wrap the fish in cheesecloth and simmer for 8 to 10 minutes per pound before baking. She served* finnan haddie *with boiled or steamed potatoes, cooked carrots, and pickled cucumber salad. The fish and potatoes would be swimming in melted butter, with finely chopped hard-cooked eggs scattered over the top. Serves 4.*

> 2 pounds *finnan haddie* (smoked haddock)
> 2 cups hot whole milk (not boiling)
> ½ cup fine dry bread crumbs
> Chopped parsley

Special equipment: cheesecloth

Preheat oven to 350 degrees. Tie the fish in cheesecloth and soak it in cold water for half an hour. Place the fish, skin side down, in a greased baking dish. Cover with hot milk. Sprinkle with bread crumbs and chopped parsley. Bake for 1 hour.

# *Fiskeboller* in Curried Cream Sauce

*Gudrun liked to add a little mild curry seasoning to the white sauce, enough to turn the cream sauce a pretty pale yellow. Serve this with boiled or steamed potatoes, cooked carrots, and flatbrød. We also enjoyed fiskeboller with a big bowl of cucumber salad, and individual salads of a leaf of lettuce, a ring of pineapple, and a dollop of cottage cheese in the middle. Serves 4, allowing 4 to 6 fish balls per person.*

> 2 tablespoons butter
> 4 tablespoons flour
> ½ teaspoon salt
> 3–4 cups hot whole milk
> 2 cans (13.7 ounces each) Norwegian fish balls,
>     such as Husmor, Bjellands, or King Oscar,
>     drained; 1½–2 cups broth reserved
> 2–3 teaspoons curry powder, to taste
> 1 teaspoon nutmeg

In a double boiler, melt butter and whisk in flour, incorporating flour thoroughly to get a smooth roux. Let cook for 3 minutes. Add salt and heated milk very slowly. Cook over medium to low heat, stirring, until thick. Add reserved broth from can of fish balls slowly while stirring. Sprinkle curry powder and nutmeg into the white sauce and stir well. Add fish balls and simmer about 15 minutes, until the fish balls are piping hot. Serve the fish balls and sauce in a heated dish.

# *Fiskeboller* in Cream Sauce with Sherry and Lobster

1 quart whole milk

8 tablespoons (1 stick) butter

2 tablespoons flour

1 teaspoon nutmeg

Pinch of salt

1 can (13.7 ounces) Norwegian fish balls,
    drained and broth reserved

2–4 tablespoons sherry

2 cans (6.5 ounces each) lobster or crab meat, chopped

Chopped fresh parsley for garnish

Heat milk in the top of a double boiler. In a separate pot, melt butter and slowly whisk in flour, nutmeg, and salt. Cook, stirring, 3 to 5 minutes. Gradually add heated milk to flour-butter mixture and stir constantly until sauce thickens. Transfer sauce along with reserved fish broth, sherry, and lobster meat back to the double boiler and simmer until the sauce is medium thick but still runny, much like a gravy. Add the fish balls to the sauce and simmer until heated through, about 15 minutes. (The fish balls can simmer longer over low heat until you are ready to eat.) Garnish with fresh parsley.

**Variation:** You may also brown the *fiskeboller* in a cast-iron frying pan with lots of butter. Place them on the serving platter and top with remaining melted butter sauce. Fried fish balls also make a fine topping for *smørbrød*. Gudrun often made fried fish balls in a hurry when unexpected company walked in the door.

# Gravlaks

*This recipe requires up to three days advance preparation and serves 8 to 10 people. You can have your fish market fillet a whole fish and use both fillets. If you do not use the whole fish, it is best to use salmon from the center of the fillet, rather than from the thinner tail end. Serve gravlaks with lots of mustard sauce, creamed diced potatoes, pickled cucumber salad with dill, lemon slices or wedges, and flatbrød. We serve this as an appetizer, or as a main course.*

3½–4 pounds salmon fillet
¼ cup sugar
¼ cup coarse kosher salt (you can substitute regular salt)
1 teaspoon white pepper
Fresh dill sprigs, a large bunch
Lemon wedges

Scrape salmon scales and wipe skin. Remove bones. Place salmon fillets, skin side down, in a deep enamel, stainless steel, or glass baking dish. (Or you can use a large rectangular plastic container with an airtight cover, which makes turning the fish easier later.)

Combine sugar, kosher salt, and pepper. Sprinkle evenly over fillets. Wash and shake dry the bunch of dill and place on top of salt mixture on the fish, reserving a few sprigs for garnish. You may want to chop the dill coarsely to release its flavor and then sprinkle over the fish.

Lay one fillet, skin side up, on top of the other. Wrap dish loosely with plastic wrap or aluminum foil and lay a heavy plate over the salmon to press it (if your plate is light, place cans on top for additional weight). Store in refrigerator for 48 hours or up to three days. Turn the fish over in the pan every 12 hours, basting it with the liquid that accumulates. (If you've put the fish in a plastic container with a tight lid, you can turn the whole container over.) Separate the halves a little to baste the salmon inside. Replace the platter and weights each time you turn the fish over.

When you are ready to serve the *gravlaks*, scrape curing mixture off the salmon. Pat the salmon dry with paper towels. Put the fillet halves skin side down on a carving board. Using a long, sharp, thin knife, cut the *gravlaks* halves slightly diagonally into ⅛-inch or paper thin slices. (The slices should be as thin as purchased sliced smoked salmon.) Detach each slice from the skin and place on a serving platter. Garnish with lemon wedges and fresh dill.

## *Gravlaks Saus* (Mustard Sauce for *Gravlaks*)

*Our extended family took a short trip to Norway in 1996, and while we were there Ingeborg ordered smoked salmon, steamed salmon, or gravlaks everywhere we went. At one of our last family meals together at my cousin Sten's home, his wife, Anne Lisa, served a beautiful platter of gravlaks with all the trimmings—including a delicious mustard sauce. Every one of us jumped for joy to see that lovely gravlaks feast. On my trip to Norway in 2009, cousin Lillemor and her husband, Gunnar, also served a gravlaks banquet, and later my cousin Gerd shared with me this recipe for mustard sauce. This recipe makes 4 servings and can be doubled. —Irene*

> 1½ tablespoons Dijon mustard or 1 tablespoon dry mustard
> 1 tablespoon sugar
> 1 tablespoon white vinegar or white wine vinegar
> 1 teaspoon salt
> ¼ teaspoon white pepper
> 1 egg yolk (optional)
> ½ cup olive oil or safflower oil
> 2–4 tablespoons chopped fresh dill, to taste (optional)

Whisk mustard, sugar, vinegar, salt, pepper, and egg yolk if using. Slowly whisk in the oil, a tiny bit at a time, until it is emulsified. Add the chopped fresh dill.

# Hot Mustard Sauce

*This sauce is good with ham, cold cuts, or gravlaks. Makes about 3 cups.*

> 4 tablespoons Dijon mustard or 4 teaspoons dry mustard
> 1 pint heavy cream, divided
> ½ cup sugar
> 3 egg yolks, beaten with ½ teaspoon salt
> 1 cup of vinegar

Blend mustard into a few tablespoons of the cream and set aside. In the top of a double boiler, bring remaining cream just to a boil. Blend in sugar, then mustard mixture. Add egg yolks and cook, stirring, 2 to 3 minutes, until eggs are cooked and the mixture is smooth. Slowly whisk in the vinegar and serve.

# Gudrun's Fish

*Serve with melted butter, chopped hard-cooked eggs, boiled or steamed new potatoes, cooked carrots, cucumber salad, and flatbrød. Serves 4.*

2 pounds firm white fish fillets, such as white fish, haddock, or cod
½ onion, sliced
1–2 tablespoons mustard seeds
1–2 tablespoons cumin seeds
1–2 teaspoons dry mustard
1 teaspoon whole black peppercorns
1 teaspoon cardamom
Sprinkle of dill
Minced parsley and dill for garnish
Lemon wedges for garnish
Melted butter for serving

Special equipment: cheesecloth

Wrap fish in cheesecloth. In a medium saucepan or fish poaching pan, add onion, mustard seeds, cumin seeds, dry mustard, peppercorns, cardamom, dill, and enough water to nearly fill the pan. Gently simmer spices at least 20 minutes and then add fish. Simmer fish for 15 minutes, then remove fish from liquid and serve on a heated platter. Sprinkle fish with parsley and dill and serve surrounded by lemon wedges. Pass melted butter in a gravy dish.

# Eddie's Fish

*After Gudrun passed away, Irving would not eat. He only wanted to taste the flavors of Gudrun's cooking. So Eddie experimented, trying to achieve the same flavors, the same tenderness, and the same delicious fish dinners. He became a master at re-creating Gudrun's way with flavors, tenderness, spice, and aroma, and his gravy was out of this world. Irving loved it.*

*Eddie's fish can be made with cod, haddock, or other firm white fish. Serve with steamed potatoes, cooked carrots, and flatbrød. We always serve this with a bowl of cucumber salad and perhaps a carrot salad, but it is also good with steamed asparagus. Serves 4 to 6.*

2 quarts water

2 tablespoons salt

2 tablespoons mustard seeds

2 tablespoons dry mustard

1 teaspoon sesame seeds

1 teaspoon whole black peppercorns

1 teaspoon whole cardamom

Sprinkle of dill

Sprinkle of ground cloves

Sprinkle of white pepper

Sprinkle of curry powder

½ onion, sliced

3 bay leaves

2–3 pounds haddock fillets (you can use the frozen fillets)

6 medium to large potatoes, peeled and cut into 2-inch chunks

6 carrots, peeled and cut into large chunks

1 package (16 ounces) frozen peas

8 tablespoons (1 stick) butter

3 chopped hard-cooked eggs

Chopped parsley

Lemon wedges

Special equipment: cheesecloth

Fill a heavy stock pot about 12 inches deep with 2 quarts water. Add the salt, mustard seeds, dry mustard, sesame seeds, peppercorns, cardamom, dill, ground cloves, white pepper, curry powder, sliced onion, and 3 bay leaves and boil for 15 minutes. Add fish fillets to spiced water, lower heat to a strong simmer, and cook 15 minutes or until fish floats.

Meanwhile, in separate pots, boil or steam the potatoes and heat the peas with carrots. Melt butter in a small saucepan or in the microwave and mix with chopped hard-cooked eggs.

When fish is cooked through, remove the fish from the broth with a broad spatula. Drain peas, carrots, and potatoes and arrange around the fish on a serving platter. Garnish with parsley, lemon wedges, and a little egg-butter mixture, reserving the rest to pass.

# Alaskan Halibut

*Serve this with lemon wedges, steamed or boiled new potatoes, and cooked peas and carrots. Broccoli, steamed asparagus, or Brussels sprouts are also good with this dish. Serves 5 to 6.*

2½ to 3 pounds halibut or other firm
    white fish (fresh or frozen fillets)
2 quarts water
1 cup celery leaves
1 onion, sliced
3 bay leaves
1 tablespoon salt
1 teaspoon thyme
½ teaspoon onion salt
½ teaspoon celery salt

**Sauce**
4 tablespoons (½ stick) butter
½ cup flour
½ teaspoon salt
¼ teaspoon celery salt
¼ teaspoon onion salt
⅛ teaspoon pepper
1 bouillon cube
2 cups reserved poaching liquid
1 cup plus 2 tablespoons whole milk
1 cup sliced mushrooms, fresh or canned,
    drained and sautéed in butter and a
    little white wine
1 cup medium or small shrimp, fresh, frozen,
    or canned
3 tablespoons sherry

Special equipment: cheesecloth

Tie fish in cheesecloth. In a large, heavy stock pot, combine 2 quarts water with celery leaves, onion, bay leaves, salt, thyme, onion salt, and celery salt and bring to a gentle simmer. Simmer for at least 20 minutes. Add fish to simmering water and poach gently for 20 minutes. Remove fish from poaching liquid and reserve 2 cups fish stock for sauce. Strain stock through a cheesecloth. Remove bone and skin from fish and cut into individual servings. Preheat oven to 350 degrees and butter a 13 by 9-inch glass baking dish.

To make the sauce, melt butter in a saucepan over low heat. Stir in flour, salt, celery salt, onion salt, and pepper. Remove from heat. Dissolve bouillon cube in reserved poaching liquid and slowly add with milk to the butter-flour mixture, stirring constantly until sauce thickens. Add sautéed mushrooms to sauce. Spread a thin layer of the sauce over the bottom of the buttered baking dish. Arrange fish in baking dish, cover with more sauce, and top each serving with three whole shrimp. Sprinkle with sherry. Cover with aluminum foil and bake 15 to 20 minutes.

# Lutefisk

*My mother always talked about how they made* lutefisk *the old-fashioned way in Norway. They would catch the codfish, soak it in lye, dry it, and then bury it in the ground. When it was time to cook it, they dug it up and soaked it in water to reconstitute it. My mother made* lutefisk *at Christmastime when we could get it from the Chicago delicatessens (she served it with* flatbrød *and boiled carrots and potatoes), and all of the Norwegian Lutheran Churches served* lutefisk *dinners at Christmastime, too. When I was living in San Francisco, my friends Julia and Darrell Huwe, who were also from the Midwest, had a* lutefisk *supper for our singles group who had not gone "home" for Christmas. I thought it tasted delicious, but I never admitted I liked* lutefisk.*

*This recipe is an old-fashioned way of making* lutefisk *that must be started about four weeks in advance. Nowadays, most people purchase* lutefisk *frozen and already reconstituted, in which case you need only keep the fish in cold water for 3 or 4 hours before baking or boiling as directed below. Serves 10.  —Irene*

> 5 pounds dried codfish
> 1 cup of washing soda (lye)
> 3 gallons boiled cooled water

Special equipment: cheesecloth, enamel pot for boiling *lutefisk* (aluminum will turn black)

Cut the fish into serving pieces. You may need to use a saw, as it is difficult to cut. Place the fish in a stone crock or a wooden tub and soak it in cold water for four days, changing the water every day. After four days, drain fish and place it in a container large enough that the fish will be covered by the boiled cooled water.

Mix washing soda with a little boiling water. Let it cool. Add soda mixture to the boiled, cooled water and pour over the cod, enough to cover. Place fish in a cold place and soak in this solution for three weeks.

Remove fish from the solution and rinse. Add fresh, cold water, and soak the fish for four more days, changing the water every day. The fish is now ready to use, but if you don't cook and eat it right away, keep it in the cold water, changing the water every day.

*If using previously frozen, thawed* lutefisk, *begin here or with baked* lutefisk, *below.*

> Salt
> Pepper
> Butter, melted

**For boiled *lutefisk*:** When ready to cook the fish, skin and wash the fillets while you bring salted water to a boil in a large enamel pot. Tie *lutefisk* in cheesecloth (the fish falls apart easily) and place in boiling salted water for 5 minutes or until it is tender. Drain fish, season with salt and pepper, and top with lots of melted butter. Serve immediately on hot plates.

**For baked *lutefisk*:** Preheat oven to 400 degrees. Line a baking pan with a large piece of aluminum foil. (The aluminum foil will turn black but won't affect the taste of the fish.) Place *lutefisk* pieces on foil and salt the fish. Fold foil over the fish like an envelope. Bake approximately 20 minutes. Remove from oven, sprinkle with salt and pepper, and serve immediately on hot plates with lots of melted butter.

# Shrimp Newburg

*Serve with rice and garnish with parsley and lemon wedges. Serves 4.*

> 1 package (1 pound) frozen cleaned
>    and deveined shrimp, defrosted in
>    cold water or refrigerator
> 1 can (10.75 ounces) condensed cream
>    of shrimp soup
> ¼ cup milk
> ½ teaspoon salt
> ¼ teaspoon ground nutmeg
> 2 egg yolks
> ¼ cup dry white wine
> Hot cooked rice

Bring a pot of water to a boil. Add thawed shrimp, cover, and turn off heat. Move shrimp to a pot of cold water, cover, and heat on medium. Test shrimp for doneness after 3 minutes (they will turn opaque and firm; cooking time depends on size of shrimp) and drain immediately when shrimp are cooked through.

Combine soup, milk, salt, and nutmeg in a separate medium saucepan and bring to a boil. In a small bowl, lightly beat egg yolks with wine. Blend about ½ cup of the hot soup mixture into the eggs, then slowly stir egg mixture into remaining sauce in saucepan. Cook, stirring constantly, over low heat for 1 minute or until slightly thickened. Add drained shrimp, stir, and serve over rice.

# Tuna Potato Bake

*This comforting dish serves 4.*

>4 cups mashed potatoes
>¼ cup milk
>1 tablespoon butter
>1 teaspoon salt
>¼ teaspoon pepper
>2 cans (7 ounces each) tuna packed
>    in water, drained
>2 eggs
>1 cup light cream or half-and-half
>3 cups grated Gruyère cheese
>1 can (6 ounces) fried onion rings

Preheat oven to 350 degrees. Butter a 2-quart casserole. Mix mashed potatoes with milk, butter, salt, and pepper. Add tuna and mix well, then spoon mixture into casserole and flatten with a spatula. In another bowl, beat eggs with cream or half-and-half and stir in cheese. Pour egg mixture over potatoes. Bake for 15 minutes and top with fried onion rings. Continue baking until casserole is nicely browned, about 20 minutes longer.

# Breads and Coffee Cakes

## Breads

Gudrun's Banana Bread

*Boller* (Norwegian Buns)

*Lefse* Made with Fresh Potatoes

*Lefse* Made with Potato Buds

Mrs. J. Dalton's Authentic Yorkshire Pudding

## Coffee Cakes

Blueberry Coffee Cake

Braided Coffee Cake

Buttery Streusel Coffee Cake

Grandmother's Coffee Ring

Nam Nam Coffee Cake

Quick Apple Coffee Cake

Rhubarb Coffee Cake

# BREADS

## Gudrun's Banana Bread

*These make very fine Christmas gifts. The sliced bread is good spread with butter or cream cheese, and it is delicious toasted. Of course, it is also good plain.*

2 cups flour
1½ teaspoons baking powder
1 teaspoon baking soda
½ teaspoon salt
4 large very ripe bananas
1 teaspoon lemon juice
1 cup sugar
½ cup shortening (not butter)
2 large eggs, room temperature
1 teaspoon vanilla extract, or more to taste
½ cup sour cream
½ cup chopped walnuts

Preheat oven to 350 degrees. Grease and flour one 10 x 6 x 2½-inch or two 7⅜ x 3⅝ x 2¼-inch loaf pans. Sift together flour, baking powder, baking soda, and salt and set aside. Mash bananas with lemon juice.

In a separate bowl, cream sugar and shortening and then add eggs and vanilla extract, using an electric hand mixer or stand mixer. Add mashed bananas, sour cream, and walnuts. Mix in sifted ingredients.

Divide batter into loaf pans or pour into one larger loaf pan. Bake for 40 minutes. Cover with foil and return to oven for an additional 10 minutes, or until a toothpick inserted in the center comes out clean. Cool in the pan on a rack for about 10 minutes before turning upside down to remove from the pan.

# *Boller* (Norwegian Buns)

*Nearly every week, Tante Asse (our father's sister) and Uncle George Moe would drive in from Chicago to see us. First they would stop at the Norwegian delicatessen and bakery on Halstead Street to buy finnan haddie, smoked mackerel, almond tarts, and boller. Eddie would mash the boller flat between his two hands before eating them. They were soft and full of cardamom aroma and flavor.*

*Begin these several hours in advance to allow for two rising periods. This recipe makes about 4 dozen.*

7 cups flour
2 envelopes (.25 ounce each) dry yeast
½ cup sugar
1 tablespoon ground cardamom
1 teaspoon salt
1 egg, lightly beaten
2 cups lukewarm milk, 105–115 degrees
2 cups raisins (optional)
8 tablespoons (1 stick) unsalted butter, melted

Stir together flour, yeast, sugar, cardamom, and salt. Mix egg, lukewarm milk, and melted butter and combine with the flour mixture. If using raisins, plump them in boiling water and then drain.

Knead dough thoroughly. Knead in raisins, if using. Cover dough loosely with a muslin dish cloth or a kitchen towel and let rise in a warm place until double in size, about 1 to 2 hours.

Grease hands and pull off pieces of dough, forming dough into rolls about 2½ to 3 inches in diameter. Place each roll on a greased cookie sheet. Let rise again until double in size.

Preheat oven to 375 degrees. Bake until rolls are light brown, approximately 15 minutes. Remove from oven and immediately brush rolls with butter.

# *Lefse* Made with Fresh Potatoes

*Lefse is a round, thin, soft potato bread—maybe ⅛ inch thick. Our lefse was about a foot in diameter. We usually spread it with soft butter, sprinkled it with sugar, and rolled it up. Sometimes we then cut the roll into little pieces, but usually we picked up the long cylinder with our hands and ate it right up. We usually ate lefser with coffee or milk as a between-meal treat, but other families ate them with their meals, rolling them up around bites of food.*

*A lefse griddle is a large round electric griddle made of Teflon or aluminum. You could also use a wide nonstick pan, cast-iron pan, or other electric griddle. If you don't have Norwegian turning sticks, a spatula is fine. The lefse rolling pin is a grooved pin, and the rolling pin cover helps prevent the dough from sticking.*

*This recipe calls for cooked potatoes, but many now use potato buds, as in the next recipe. Both variations are delicious.*

>   5½ cups cooked russet potatoes, mashed or riced
>   ½ cup scalded milk
>   3 tablespoons melted butter
>   2 teaspoons salt
>   About 2 cups flour

Special equipment: *lefse* grill, *lefse* turning sticks (optional), *lefse* rolling pin with rolling pin cover, pastry cloth

Combine mashed potatoes with milk, butter, and salt, and mix well. Let cool, uncovered. Mix flour into potatoes and use your hands to form dough into a roll. Use as little flour as possible—just enough to hold the potatoes together. Cut dough into 10 equal portions, cover, and refrigerate until just before rolling out each *lefse*.

Turn on the *lefse* griddle and heat to 425 to 450 degrees. Roll out one portion of dough on a lightly floured pastry cloth until very thin. Place on a *lefse* griddle or pan and cook about 30 seconds, until light brown spots appear. Turn over with a *lefse* turning stick or spatula and repeat on the other side. Repeat with remaining dough, placing each cooked round between clean dish towels to cool while keeping them moist. When they are cool, fold each *lefse* into quarters.

# *Lefse* Made with Potato Buds

*This recipe is adapted from the one given to all who enjoyed their freshly made* lefse *at the Sons of Norway Christmas bazaars in the Washington, D.C., area. According to David Hofstad's family, this family recipe was used by Alice Hofstad, a fourth-generation Norwegian American from Madison, Minnesota, and a descendant of an 1843 immigrant from Nes Parish in Telemark. David has made some minor changes to his mother's recipe over the years.*

*You will need to allow several hours for chilling the dough.*

> 6 cups (one 13.75-ounce box) potato buds (not flakes)
> 10 tablespoons (1¼ sticks) butter or margarine
> ½ cup milk
> 4 teaspoons sugar
> 2 teaspoons salt
> 4½ cups boiling water
> 1½ to 1¾ cups white flour

Special equipment: *lefse* turning stick or narrow spatula, pastry board, pastry cloth, pastry board cover, electric griddle, rolling pin, cloth rolling pin cover

Pour the instant potato buds into a large metal pot or metal mixing bowl. Bring a pot of water to a boil.

In the top of a double boiler on medium heat or in a microwave, melt the butter or margarine in ½ cup milk, being careful not to let the milk boil or curdle. Stir sugar and salt into butter or margarine and milk.

Measure out 4½ cups boiling water and combine this with the butter-milk mixture, then pour mixture over potato buds in the pot and stir to combine. Knead the potato dough thoroughly until blended, then cover and chill in the refrigerator 30 to 45 minutes. Dough should still be a bit warm when you remove it from the refrigerator.

Remove the dough from the refrigerator and, while the dough is still slightly warm, knead in 1½ to 1¾ cups of flour until dough is smooth and hangs together enough to be rolled out without sticking to the pastry cloth. Form the dough into the shape of a long baguette and cut it into 24 equal pieces. (Start by cutting the dough in half. Cut each half in half again, and then cut those four pieces into halves, giving you 8 pieces. Cut each of those eighths into 3 pieces, and you will have 24 equal-sized pieces.) Roll each piece of dough into a ball.

Turn on the *lefse* griddle and heat to 425 to 450 degrees. The griddle should be hot enough to brown the *lefser* quickly without burning them. If you don't have a *lefse* grill, use a large cast-iron frying pan to make smaller *lefser*. Stack two thin cotton dish towels, about 36 inches square, on the counter next to the griddle. (You can fold the dish towels several times to make them closer to the size of the finished *lefser*.)

Attach the cloth pastry cover to the pastry board and sprinkle with additional white flour. Flatten one of the balls of *lefse* dough onto the board and begin to roll it out into a circular shape. After a few rolls of the pin, sprinkle rolled-out dough with flour, turn it over with a turning stick, and, while holding the turning stick, use your other hand to sprinkle more flour on the pastry board. Then flip the dough onto the pastry board and continue rolling it out. Sprinkle a bit more flour on the *lefse* and on the cloth rolling pin cover and continue rolling. The dough should be as thin as possible and as wide as your griddle or pan will permit. Turn the dough just once on the pastry board before you transfer it to the griddle.

Place *lefse* on the griddle and cook 30 seconds. Turn the *lefse* on the griddle at least once per side, or until it has cooked twice on each side. Sometimes cooking three times per side is needed before light brown speckles appear on the *lefse*. (Be sure to scrape off any dough that accumulates on the turning stick, or the *lefse* will stick to the turning stick and may tear as you are trying to turn it.) Use the spatula to puncture any bubbles that rise in the *lefse* as it cooks. (If the *lefse* does bubble up, that is a good thing. This means that the *lefse* has just the right consistency. Allow the little bubbles to form and pop only the big bubbles.)

As you finish each *lefse*, place it on a towel and fold the towel over it. Continue to stack the baked *lefser* one on top of the other, on half of the towel space, folding the other half of the towels over the *lefser*, to keep them completely enshrouded by the dish towels so they stay moist. If you want the *lefser* to cool more quickly, line up several towels and place the *lefser* in a single layer to cool, covered by more towels.

### *Lefse* Tips

- The thinner the *lefse*, the better. It should be just thick enough to hang together as you move it to the griddle on the *lefse* turning stick.

- If you can handle the dough and your rolling surface and griddle are large enough, you can gradually reduce the number and increase the size of the pieces of dough.

- *Lefse* baking is time consuming; most of the time is taken up with rolling out and baking each piece. The bigger your rolled-out pieces of dough, the less time you spend rolling them out and baking them. The baking will go even more quickly if one person rolls out the dough while another does the baking.

- Some people like to keep half of the dough pieces cooling in the refrigerator while baking the others. Observe whether you have better luck handling the dough if the dough is cool or at room temperature. David Hofstad has found that the dough rolls out better if it is at room temperature. Therefore, after he has completed forming the dough into balls, he lets the dough balls warm to room temperature for an hour or more. The dough should still be rather warm while you are kneading the flour into it.

- Add as little flour as possible to the dough during the rolling-out process. The baked *lefse* will be tastier this way. But sprinkle a little flour on the covered pastry board every time you turn the *lefse* over, and again before you begin rolling out another piece of dough.

- You can vary the amount of butter or margarine, from as little as ¼ cup to ¾ cup, for a softer, tastier *lefse*.

☙ When you slide the turning stick under the *lefse* to lift it up before adding more flour and turning the *lefse* (or putting it on the griddle), insert the stick under the near edge about one-third of the way across the *lefse*, lifting the handle of the stick so that the tip angles into the pastry cloth a little. Slowly push it far enough so that the tip sticks out the other side about an inch. Carefully lift and roll the stick slightly toward the center so the nearest edge lifts; then lift and roll the stick into the center before lifting the *lefse* completely off the board.

☙ David aims for a perfectly round piece of *lefse* every time. But he says he always has two sharp knives handy while he is rolling out *lefser*; he uses one of them to trim the pieces he has rolled out if they are lopsided or irregular. (He uses the second knife to scrape off the dough that tends to accumulate on the first knife.)

☙ *Lefser* are best eaten soon after they are baked, but they can be frozen. You can warm them up in the microwave for a few seconds after they have thawed out.

# Mrs. J. Dalton's Authentic Yorkshire Pudding

*Gudrun made friends everywhere she went. When she and Irene took the ship to Europe—destination Norway—in 1963 and took additional sea transportation between Ireland, England, and Denmark, Gudrun struck up a conversation with a British woman. The woman, as it turned out, hailed from Yorkshire, England, and their friendly chat inevitably turned to trading recipes. This authentic Yorkshire pudding recipe was the result, and whenever she served it, Gudrun credited her West Yorkshire friend, the good Mrs. J. Dalton of the City of Leeds.*

*This makes one Yorkshire pudding about the size of a 6- to 9-inch Bundt pan. You can also make it in a bread pan, a 6- to 8-inch glass dish, or as individual popovers in a greased muffin pan. If making popovers, reduce the baking time to about 10 minutes or until puffed and golden brown.*

> 4 large tablespoons flour
> ½ teaspoon salt
> Pinch of pepper
> 2 eggs
> Touch of milk
> Touch of cold water

Preheat the oven to 450 degrees. Generously grease a round, deep cake pan or a 9-inch glass or cast-iron casserole.

In a large bowl, combine flour, salt, and pepper. Make a well in the center and add eggs to well. Beat eggs with a whisk, slowly incorporating flour mixture until thoroughly mixed, and gradually add a little milk and cold water until you obtain a thick batter.

Heat the greased baking dish in the oven until very hot. Pour in batter and return dish to oven. Bake until mixture is well risen and brown, about 30 minutes.

## COFFEE CAKES

# Blueberry Coffee Cake

*Makes 2 cakes, 9 to 12 servings each.*

**Topping**

1 cup sugar

⅔ cup flour

8 tablespoons (1 stick) butter, softened

1 teaspoon cinnamon

**Batter**

4 cups flour

1½ cups sugar

1½ cups milk

½ cup shortening

1 tablespoon plus 2 teaspoons baking powder

1½ teaspoons salt

2 eggs

4 cups fresh or frozen blueberries

**Glaze**

2 cups confectioners' sugar

4 tablespoons (½ stick) butter, softened

1 teaspoon vanilla extract

⅓–½ cup water or milk

Preheat oven to 375 degrees. Grease two 9-inch round or square cake pans.

Combine the topping ingredients and set aside. To make the batter, mix all batter ingredients except blueberries until moistened. Beat vigorously by hand or with an electric mixer for an additional 30 seconds. Carefully stir in blueberries. Spread half of the batter in each pan; sprinkle with topping and bake until a toothpick inserted in the center comes out clean, 45 to 50 minutes. Cool slightly.

While the cake is baking, make the glaze. Mix confectioners' sugar, butter, and vanilla extract in a medium-size bowl. Stir in ⅓ to ½ cup water or milk, about 2 tablespoons at a time, until glaze is of spreading consistency. When the cake is slightly cooled, drizzle glaze on top. Serve warm.

# Braided Coffee Cake

*Start this recipe several hours or the day before. Makes 3 cakes.*

> 2 cakes (2 ounces each) compressed yeast
> 1¼ cups warm milk
> 2 eggs
> ½ teaspoon vanilla extract
> 4 cups flour
> 2 tablespoons sugar
> 1 teaspoon salt
> ½ pound (2 sticks) butter
> 1 cup candied citron or 1 cup drained, canned
>     mandarin oranges, with each section
>     cut into 2 to 4 pieces
> ½ cup raisins

Dissolve yeast in warm milk; blend in eggs and vanilla. In a separate bowl, cut flour, sugar, and salt into butter as for pie crust, then add to yeast mixture along with fruit and raisins. Mix thoroughly and refrigerate 4 hours or overnight.

Divide dough into nine portions. Roll each portion out into a strip about 6 inches long. Braid three at a time, making three braided cakes. Sprinkle cakes with water and let rise 2 hours.

Preheat oven to 350 degrees and bake 40 minutes to 1 hour, until a toothpick inserted in the center comes out clean.

# Buttery Streusel Coffee Cake

*Makes 2 cakes, 9 to 12 servings each.*

**Cinnamon Nut Filling**
½ cup firmly packed brown sugar
½ cup finely chopped nuts
2 teaspoons cinnamon

**Streusel Topping**
1 cup sugar
8 tablespoons (1 stick) chilled butter
½ cup flour

**Confectioners' Glaze**
2 cups confectioners' sugar
4 tablespoons (½ stick) butter, softened
1 teaspoon vanilla extract
⅓–½ cup water or milk

**Batter**
3 cups flour
1½ cups sugar
1½ cups milk
½ cup shortening
1 tablespoon plus 2 teaspoons
    baking powder
1½ teaspoons salt
2 eggs

Make the cinnamon nut filling by mixing brown sugar, nuts, and cinnamon in a small bowl; set aside.

To make the streusel topping, use a pastry blender or handheld electric mixer to combine sugar, butter, and flour until crumbly. Set aside.

To make the confectioners' glaze, mix confectioners' sugar, softened butter, and vanilla extract in a medium-size bowl. Stir in water or milk about 2 tablespoons at a time, until glaze is of spreading consistency. Set aside.

Preheat oven to 375 degrees. Grease two 9-inch round or square cake pans. Using an electric mixer, combine all batter ingredients until moistened; beat vigorously for an additional 30 seconds. (Gudrun was so strong that she often beat it by hand with a big fork.) Spread about 1⅓ cups batter in each pan (you should still have about ⅔ cup batter remaining). Sprinkle half the cinnamon nut filling over the batter in each pan and divide the remaining batter between the pans. Sprinkle with topping. Bake until a toothpick inserted in the center comes out clean, 30 to 35 minutes. Cool slightly. Drizzle confectioners' glaze on top. Serve warm.

# Grandmother's Coffee Ring

**Batter**

4 eggs

½ cup sugar

8 tablespoons (1 stick) butter,
    melted and cooled

½ cup raisins

½ cup citron, finely chopped, or
    2 tablespoons grated lemon zest

½ teaspoon almond extract

2½ cups flour, sifted five times

1 tablespoon baking powder

1 teaspoon salt

½ teaspoon ground cardamom

**Topping**

1 egg

1 cup confectioners' sugar

½ teaspoon almond extract

1 package (8 ounces) sweetened,
    flaked coconut

Preheat oven to 350 degrees. Grease a cookie sheet. Beat eggs with sugar. Add melted butter, raisins, citron or grated lemon zest, and almond extract. Sift together previously sifted flour, baking powder, salt, and cardamom, then gradually add sifted dry ingredients to egg mixture and stir to combine. Spoon the dough into a round ring on greased cookie sheet. Bake for 20 minutes.

While cake is baking, make the topping. Beat egg with confectioners' sugar and ½ teaspoon almond extract. Fold in coconut. Spread topping over cake and bake an additional 10 minutes or until a toothpick inserted in the center comes out clean.

# Nam Nam Coffee Cake

*In our family, we often said "nam nam" to mean, "This is so delicious, I can hardly wait for the next bite!"*

**Batter**

2 cups flour, sifted

1 teaspoon baking powder

1 teaspoon baking soda

½ teaspoon salt

8 tablespoons (1 stick) butter, softened

1 cup sugar

2 eggs

1 cup sour cream

1 teaspoon vanilla extract

**Topping/Filling**

1 cup granulated sugar

1 cup brown sugar

1 cup chopped walnuts, chopped pecans,
    or blueberries, or a combination totaling
    1 cup (all three are optional)

1 teaspoon cinnamon

Preheat oven to 325 degrees. Sift together previously sifted flour, baking powder, baking soda, and salt. In a separate bowl, cream butter and sugar with an electric mixer. Add eggs while mixing. Little by little, add flour mixture. Add sour cream and vanilla extract. Mix well. In a separate bowl, combine topping/filling ingredients.

Starting with batter and ending with topping, alternate two layers each of topping and batter in a 9 x 9-inch cake pan. Bake 40 minutes or until a toothpick inserted in the center comes out clean.

# Quick Apple Coffee Cake

*This simple sugar-and-cinnamon-topped cake is especially good when served warm with whipped cream.*

**Batter**

8 tablespoons (1 stick) butter, softened

1 cup sugar

2 eggs

2 teaspoons vanilla extract

2 cups flour, sifted

3 teaspoons baking powder

¼ teaspoon salt

¾ cup milk

**Topping**

¼ cup sugar

1 tablespoon cinnamon

3 cups peeled and sliced apples (about 6 tart, crisp apples)

Preheat oven to 350 degrees. Grease and flour two 9-inch round cake pans. Cream butter and sugar. Add eggs and vanilla extract and blend well.

In another bowl, combine flour, baking powder, and salt. Alternating with milk, add dry ingredients to egg mixture, stirring until smooth. In a separate bowl, blend sugar and cinnamon for the topping.

Pour batter into prepared cake pans. Arrange apple slices on top. Sprinkle cinnamon-sugar mixture over apples and bake 35 to 40 minutes or until a toothpick inserted in the center comes out clean.

# Rhubarb Coffee Cake

*If you do not have sour milk or lemon juice called for in this recipe, you can leave out the sour milk, but increase the buttermilk to 2 cups.*

### Batter
1 cup brown sugar
½ cup shortening
2 eggs, lightly beaten
2 cups flour
1 teaspoon baking soda
¼ teaspoon salt
1 cup buttermilk
1 cup sour milk (1 teaspoon lemon juice plus 1 cup milk)
1 teaspoon vanilla extract
2 cups diced rhubarb

### Topping
1 cup brown sugar
1 teaspoon cinnamon

Preheat oven to 350 degrees and grease and flour a 9 x 9-inch pan. Using an electric mixer, cream brown sugar and shortening. Add eggs to shortening mixture and combine. Add flour, baking soda, and salt. Stir in buttermilk, sour milk, and vanilla extract and mix thoroughly. Stir in rhubarb and pour batter into prepared pan.

Combine topping ingredients and sprinkle over batter. Bake 45 minutes or until a toothpick inserted in the center comes out clean.

# Cakes and Tortes

Fruit Cocktail Torte

Gudrun's Apricot Sponge Cake Torte

Applesauce Cake

*Bløtkake* (Norwegian Birthday Cake or
    Whipped Cream Layer Cake)

Carrot Cake

Gudrun's Frosted Chocolate Cake

Coffee Cloud Cake

Dundee Cakes

Easy Almond Cake

French Apple Cake

*Fyrstekake* (Prince Cake)

*Fyrstekake med Epler* (Prince Cake with Apples)

Heath Candy (Fruit Cake)

Honey Cake

*Julekake*

*Kransekake* (Norwegian Ring Cake) Made
    with Fresh Almonds

*Kransekake* Made with Almond Paste

Mama's Cake

Orange Spice Cake

Walnut Cake

# Fruit Cocktail Torte

1½ cups flour

1 cup sugar

1 teaspoon baking powder

1 teaspoon baking soda

¼ teaspoon salt

1 egg, beaten

1 can (15 ounces) fruit cocktail with juice

1 cup brown sugar

1 cup chopped nuts

Preheat oven to 350 degrees. Grease a 9 x 13-inch pan. Sift together flour, sugar, baking powder, baking soda, and salt. In a separate bowl, combine egg and fruit cocktail. Fold in dry ingredients. Pour into prepared pan. Top with brown sugar and nuts. Bake for 45 minutes or until a toothpick inserted in the center comes out clean.

# Gudrun's Apricot Sponge Cake Torte

**Batter**

3 eggs, room temperature

1 cup sugar

1 teaspoon almond extract

1 teaspoon vanilla extract

¼ teaspoon salt

½ cup flour

½ scant cup potato flour

2 teaspoons baking powder

5 tablespoons juice reserved from
   canned apricots below

**Apricot Filling**

1 can (20 ounces) apricots, drained
   and juice reserved

½ pint (1 cup) whipping cream

**Cream Filling**

2 cups milk

3 egg yolks

⅔ cup sugar

⅓ cup flour

1 tablespoon rum extract

**Topping**

Whipping cream

2 tablespoons confectioners' sugar

2 teaspoons vanilla extract

Preheat oven to 350 degrees. Grease and flour two 8- or 9-inch round cake pans. Beat eggs until thick. Add sugar, almond extract, vanilla extract, and salt. In a separate bowl, sift together dry ingredients. Alternating, add flour mixture and apricot juice to egg mixture. Pour batter into cake pans (layers will be thin) and bake for 15 minutes or until a toothpick inserted in the center comes out clean.

While the cake is baking, make the fillings and topping. To make the apricot filling, mash canned apricots and fold in whipped cream.

To make the cream filling, bring the milk to a boil in the top of a double boiler. In a separate bowl, mix egg yolks, sugar, and flour, beating with an electric hand mixer. Add ¼ cup hot milk to egg mixture. Pour mixture into pot with remaining 1¾ cups hot milk and cook until thick, stirring constantly. Let mixture cool into a custard, then add rum extract.

To make the topping, whip the cream with confectioners' sugar and vanilla extract until soft peaks form.

When the cake has cooled, spread one layer first with apricot filling, then with cream filling. Place the second cake layer on top and repeat. Top cake with sweetened whipped cream.

# Applesauce Cake

8 tablespoons (1 stick) butter
1 cup sugar
2 eggs
2 cups sifted flour
1 cup applesauce
1 cup sour cream
1 teaspoon vanilla extract
1 teaspoon baking powder
1 teaspoon cinnamon
1 teaspoon baking soda
½ teaspoon salt

Preheat oven to 350 degrees. Grease a 8½ x 5½ x 2½-inch loaf pan. With an electric mixer, cream together butter and sugar. Beat in eggs. Stir in remaining ingredients. Pour batter into pan and bake for 30 minutes or until a toothpick inserted in the center comes out clean.

# *Bløtkake* (Norwegian Birthday Cake, or Whipped Cream Layer Cake)

*You can top this with strawberries or other fruits, and, if desired, you can substitute rum filling (see Mama's Cake, page 172, for recipe) for the butter cream. Allow time to chill the cake layers overnight. (Very cold cake layers make it easier to spread the filling between each layer.)*

**Batter**

1¼ cups sifted cake flour

2 teaspoons double-acting
    baking powder

6 eggs, separated

¾ cup sugar

**Butter Cream Filling with Chocolate Shavings**

3 squares semisweet chocolate

12 tablespoons (1½ sticks) butter

1¼ cups confectioners' sugar

2 eggs

**Frosting**

2 cups heavy whipping cream

½ cup confectioners' sugar

2 teaspoons vanilla extract

Preheat oven to 325 degrees. Line the bottoms of three 9-inch round cake pans with parchment paper.

To make the batter, sift previously sifted flour with baking powder. In a small mixing bowl, beat 6 egg yolks with ¾ cup sugar on high speed until light. Fold beaten yolks into the flour mixture using an electric hand mixer on low.

In a large bowl, beat 6 egg whites until stiff. Fold the beaten egg whites into flour-yolk mixture using a rubber spatula. Gently pour into pans. Bake 15 minutes or until golden and a toothpick inserted in the center comes out clean. Cool, inverted, on racks for 10 to 15 minutes. Remove from pans, wrap in plastic or waxed paper, and freeze overnight.

Using a knife, shred chocolate squares and set aside. In a small bowl, mix, at high speed, the butter, confectioners' sugar, and 2 eggs until creamy. Chill for 30 minutes.

To make the frosting, whip heavy cream with confectioners' sugar and vanilla extract. Chill constantly until ready to frost the cake.

Thaw wrapped cakes at room temperature 1 hour. On one plate, place one layer, bottom side up; spread with half of butter cream filling, then sprinkle with one-third of shredded chocolate. Place second layer and repeat filling and chocolate, then place third layer (you should still have one-third of the chocolate shavings in reserve). Frost entire cake with whipped cream frosting and garnish with reserved chocolate shavings. Refrigerate until ready to serve.

# Carrot Cake

*Gudrun always saved the waxed paper wrapping from store-bought butter. Any remaining butter on the wrappers was used to grease the cake pans. We called these papers the "already-buttered butter papers."*

> 2 eggs
> 1 cup safflower oil
> 1 scant cup sugar
> 1 teaspoon cinnamon
> 1 teaspoon vanilla extract
> ½ teaspoon salt
> 2½ cups flour
> 2 cups finely grated raw carrots
> 1 cup unsweetened crushed pineapple, drained
> ⅔ cup chopped pecans

Preheat oven to 325 degrees. Grease and flour a 9 x 13-inch pan.

Combine eggs, oil, sugar, cinnamon, vanilla extract, and salt and mix well. Add flour, carrots, and pineapple and combine. Stir in pecans. Bake 60 minutes or until a toothpick inserted in the center comes out clean. This cake does not need icing.

# Gudrun's Frosted Chocolate Cake

*Eddie loved chocolate. He loved Gudrun's chocolate cake with double chocolate frosting. He loved brownies. He loved hot chocolate made from scratch. He loved chocolate graham-cracker-crust chiffon pie and chocolate chip cookies, and his fudge was divine. When he was about seven years old, he wanted to make his own recipe book, so he filled a brown spiral notebook with recipes in his own printing for all of these goodies and more. Our parents saved that cookbook for the rest of their lives.*

**Batter**

2 squares unsweetened chocolate

8 tablespoons (1 stick) butter,
    room temperature

1 cup sugar

2 large eggs, room temperature

1½ cups flour

1 teaspoon baking powder

1 teaspoon baking soda

½ teaspoon salt

2–3 teaspoons vanilla extract, to taste

1 cup sour cream

**Chocolate Frosting**

8 tablespoons (1 stick) butter, softened

2 squares unsweetened chocolate

2–3 teaspoons vanilla extract

Pinch of salt

1 teaspoon mint extract (optional)

2 cups confectioners' sugar

4–5 tablespoons whole milk or cream

Whipped cream

Preheat oven to 350 degrees. Grease and flour two 8- or 9-inch round cake pans. Melt chocolate in the top of a double boiler and cool.

While chocolate cools, cream butter, sugar, and eggs. Sift together twice the flour, baking powder, baking soda, and salt. Add chocolate and vanilla extract to butter mixture. Alternating, add a tablespoon at a time of flour mixture and sour cream to butter mixture while folding with electric hand mixer or beater. Pour batter into prepared pans. Bake 25 to 30 minutes (do not place cake pans too close together), or until a toothpick inserted in the center comes out clean. Allow cakes to cool on wire racks before turning upside down to remove from pan and before frosting.

While the cake is baking, make the frosting. Melt butter and chocolate together in the top of a double boiler. Add vanilla extract and salt. If desired, stir in mint extract. Beat on low with an electric mixer, gradually adding confectioners' sugar. Add milk or cream. Place frosting in the refrigerator to set for about 30 minutes or until cool.

When frosting has cooled, assemble the cake. Place one layer, bottom side up, on a cake plate and spread the top with a layer of frosting. Place the second cake layer on top, bottom side up. Spread remaining frosting over top and sides of cake.

**Variation:** Gudrun often made this recipe into cupcakes that had a high mound of frosting—about one-third as high as the cake! She usually kept several dozen in the freezer so that if our friends came over they could have a frozen chocolate cupcake with chocolate frosting.

For another option, you can whip 1 pint of whipped cream and add half of it to the chocolate frosting before frosting the cake or cupcakes. Use the rest to decorate the cake.

# Coffee Cloud Cake

**Batter**
2 cups sifted flour
3 teaspoons double-acting baking powder
½ teaspoon salt
6 eggs, separated
½ teaspoon cream of tartar
2 cups granulated sugar, divided
2 teaspoons vanilla extract
1 tablespoon instant coffee dissolved in 1 cup boiling
    water and cooled (or 1 cup strong coffee, cooled)
1 cup chopped walnuts

**Coffee Frosting**
9 tablespoons butter, softened
1¼ cups confectioners' sugar
2 tablespoons instant coffee
4 tablespoons heavy cream

Preheat oven to 350 degrees. Sift together flour, baking powder, and salt and set aside.

In a large bowl, beat the egg whites with cream of tartar until soft peaks begin to form. Add ½ cup of the granulated sugar, 2 tablespoons at a time, continuing to beat until stiff peaks form. Do not underbeat. Set aside.

In another large bowl, beat the egg yolks until blended. Then gradually beat in vanilla extract and remaining 1½ cups granulated sugar. Beat at high speed until mixture is thick and lemon-colored, about 5 minutes. Add flour mixture and then the cooled coffee. Fold in walnuts. Gently fold egg yolk mixture into egg white mixture. Bake in a tube pan for 60 to 70 minutes or until a toothpick inserted in the center comes out clean. Leave the cake in the pan until cooled.

Make frosting by blending together all ingredients with an electric mixer. When cake has cooled, invert pan, place cake on a serving plate, and frost.

# Dundee Cakes

*These cakes must be started several hours ahead to allow time for the fruit to marinate.*
*Makes 4 loaves or 1 tube cake.*

> 1 cup golden raisins
> 1 cup dried currants
> ½ cup chopped mixed candied fruit
> 1 teaspoon finely chopped candied ginger
> ¼ cup brandy or golden rum
> 2 tablespoons orange juice
> ½ pound (2 sticks) butter
> 1 cup sugar
> 5 eggs
> ½ cup coarsely ground blanched almonds
> 2½ cups flour
> 1 teaspoon baking powder
> ½ teaspoon salt
> 1 tablespoon grated orange rind
> Almond halves
> Citron strips
> Candied cherries

Several hours before baking time, combine raisins, currants, candied mixed fruit, and candied ginger in a small container with an airtight lid. Mix brandy or rum and orange juice and pour over the fruit. Cover tightly and marinate for 3 to 4 hours, turning upside down frequently. Drain fruit well and reserve any excess liquid for batter.

Preheat oven to 275 degrees. Grease four 6 x 3½-inch loaf pans or one tube pan. Cream butter and sugar. Beat in eggs one at a time. Stir in ground almonds. In a separate bowl, sift together flour, baking powder, and salt three times. Add drained fruit to the flour mixture and blend with a fork to coat and separate the fruit pieces.

Carefully stir flour and fruit combination into the butter mixture. Stir in the orange rind. Stir in any leftover liquid from the marinade (or add 2 tablespoons of juice or brandy or golden rum).

Pour batter into prepared pans, pressing down on the batter with the back of a spoon or spatula to eliminate air bubbles. Decorate with almond halves, citron strips, and candied cherries. Fill a shallow pan with an inch of water and place this pan on the floor of the oven. Place cake pans in the middle of the oven and bake about 1 hour. Remove water pan after an hour and bake cake for an additional 15 minutes or until a toothpick inserted in the center comes out clean.

# Easy Almond Cake

*Serve with ice cream or as coffee cake.*

> 1 cup cake flour
> ½ teaspoon baking soda
> 4 tablespoons (½ stick) butter
> 1 cup sugar
> 1 teaspoon almond extract
> ¼ teaspoon salt
> 2 eggs
> ½ cup sour cream
> 2–3 tablespoons sliced almonds

Preheat oven to 350 degrees. Grease a 9 x 9-inch pan or a fluted almond cake pan. Stir together flour and baking soda. In a separate bowl, beat butter, sugar, almond extract, and salt until mixture is lemon yellow. Add eggs and combine, beating with the electric hand mixer. Alternating, blend sour cream and flour mixture into butter mixture. Pour batter into pan and sprinkle with almonds. Bake 25 to 30 minutes or until a toothpick inserted in the center comes out clean.

# French Apple Cake

*This "cake" is more like an apple betty. If you want something more cakelike, you can add 2 eggs to the batter, but bake the cake in a large springform pan.*

> 2 cups sugar
>
> 8 tablespoons (1 stick) butter, softened
>
> 4 cups peeled diced apples (about 8 large, crisp, tart apples)
>
> 2 cups sifted flour
>
> 2 teaspoons baking soda
>
> 1 teaspoon cinnamon
>
> ½ teaspoon salt
>
> ½ teaspoon nutmeg
>
> ½ cup chopped pecans

Preheat oven to 325 degrees. Grease a 9-inch round or square pan. Cream together sugar and butter. Stir in diced apples. Add flour, baking soda, cinnamon, salt, and nutmeg and mix well. Stir in pecans. Bake 1 hour or until toothpick inserted in the center comes out clean.

# *Fyrstekake* (Prince Cake)

*The crust mixture for this cake will need to refrigerate for about 2 hours before rolling, filling, and baking.*

**Filling**

1 cup almond paste or 1 cup
    finely ground almonds
2 egg yolks
½ cup granulated sugar
½ cup confectioners' sugar, plus
    more for dusting pan
4 tablespoons (½ stick) butter
2 teaspoons almond extract
Pinch of salt
⅓–½ cup raspberry jam

**Crust**

1½ cups flour
1 egg
8 tablespoons (1 stick)
    butter
2 tablespoons sugar
1 teaspoon vanilla
Pinch of salt

In a large mixing bowl, combine all filling ingredients except raspberry jam and mix into a paste. Refrigerate.

In a separate bowl, combine the crust ingredients and refrigerate for 2 hours.

Preheat oven to 350 degrees. Grease an 8-inch round cake pan or springform pan and sprinkle with confectioners' sugar. Roll out crust mixture thinly, like pie crust. Gently lay crust in the bottom and up the sides of the pan, trimming any excess and reserving scraps. Spread raspberry jam on bottom crust. Then add almond paste filling over jam. Trim reserved crust dough into strips and crisscross over the top of the almond paste filling.

Bake for 15 minutes at 350 degrees, then lower heat to 325 degrees for 20 to 25 minutes, until crust is golden brown and a toothpick inserted in the center comes out clean.

# *Fyrstekake med Epler* (Prince Cake with Apples)

    ½ cup sugar
    8 tablespoons (1 stick) butter
    1 egg
    1 cup flour
    2 teaspoons baking powder
    1 teaspoon vanilla extract
    1 large Granny Smith, Jonathan, Gala, or other crisp,
        tart apple, peeled and diced
    Additional sugar for sprinkling on top

Preheat oven to 350 degrees. Cream sugar and butter. Add egg, flour, baking powder, and vanilla extract to creamed butter mixture and stir until it forms a dough. Press dough into a 9-inch cake pan and place apples on top. Sprinkle with sugar. Bake until cake is golden brown and a toothpick inserted in the center comes out clean, about 45 minutes.

# Heath Candy (Fruit Cake)

*This rich fruit cake must be made 2 weeks in advance to allow the flavors to ripen.*

> 3 cups sugar
> 1½ cups heavy cream
> 2 tablespoons butter
> 1 pound dried dates
> 1 pound dried figs
> 1 pound raisins
> 1 pound shredded coconut
> 1–2 cups chopped walnuts or pecans

In a heavy-bottomed saucepan over medium-high heat, cook sugar, cream, and butter to soft-ball stage. (Soft-ball stage is reached when a small amount of the mixture dropped into cold water forms a small, flexible ball, or when the mixture reaches 235–240 degrees on a candy thermometer.) Using a wooden spoon or an electric mixer on low, beat until creamy. Stir in fruits, nuts, and coconut, mixing thoroughly. Remove from heat and cool for about 10 minutes. Pour mixture out onto a clean cutting board and roll into a cylinder. Wrap the cylinder in a dampened cloth (cheesecloth or a kitchen towel), then in waxed paper. Let it "ripen" for two weeks in the refrigerator for the flavors to combine and more flavor to come out. After ripening, cut the cake into thin slices to serve.

# Honey Cake

¾ cup shortening or vegetable oil,
  or 12 tablespoons (1½) sticks butter
1 cup sugar
4 eggs, separated
1 cup honey
2½ cups flour
2 teaspoons baking powder
1 teaspoon cinnamon
1 teaspoon nutmeg
Pinch of salt
1 teaspoon baking soda
½ cup strong coffee, cooled
½ cup orange juice
½ cup slivered almonds

Preheat oven to 325 degrees. Grease a 9 x 13-inch pan. Cream shortening and sugar with an electric mixer. Add unbeaten egg yolks, then honey. In a separate bowl, sift flour with baking powder, cinnamon, nutmeg, and salt.

Dissolve baking soda in coffee. Alternating, add flour mixture to the batter, then a bit of coffee, then a bit of the orange juice, all while mixing.

In another bowl, beat egg whites until stiff; gently fold them into batter. Fold in nuts. Pour batter into pan and bake 50 minutes or until a toothpick inserted in the center comes out clean.

# Julekake

*This was a Christmas treat we all looked forward to. For most snack times, or as people came in for coffee, Gudrun would slice the julekake and spread good creamery butter on each slice. We had this in various sizes and shapes: sometimes a large oval, and sometimes a formed loaf. Julekake is a sweet bread, but not too sweet. We ate slice after slice. (Sometimes our tantes would bring ready-made loaves from a Norwegian delicatessen in Chicago. It did not take long for us to finish off an entire loaf of that, either.)*

2 envelopes (.75 ounce each) yeast
½ cup warm water
1¾ cups plus ½ teaspoon sugar, divided
½ pound (2 sticks) butter
2 cups milk, heated to lukewarm
4 cups flour
1 teaspoon ground cardamom
¼ teaspoon salt
2 eggs
2 cups raisins
1 cup candied citron

Dissolve yeast in ½ cup warm water with ½ teaspoon sugar and let stand until mixture is foamy. In a small saucepan over very low heat, melt butter in lukewarm milk.

In a separate bowl, sift together flour, 1¾ cups sugar, cardamom, and salt. Alternating, add eggs and milk-butter mixture. Add the yeast mixture and combine thoroughly. Let dough rise until it doubles in size, 1 to 2 hours.

Preheat oven to 400 degrees. Turn out dough onto lightly floured surface and knead briefly, about 10 minutes. Knead in the raisins and citron. Divide dough into two pieces and shape into two rounds. Place both rounds on a large cookie sheet. Let rise again for 15 to 20 minutes. Bake about 45 minutes or until *julekake* is golden brown and springs back when you touch it or a toothpick inserted in the center comes out clean.

# *Kransekake* (Norwegian Ring Cake) Made with Fresh Almonds

*I have made this cake for many weddings of neighborhood friends, a nephew, and, once, for the son of my first cousin one time removed when his mother came for his wedding in the United States several years ago. But I have a lot of failed kransekake stories. Once, in Boulder, Colorado, I made two kransekaker for Eddie's son Erik and his wife, Martha. I got the idea of mixing the almond paste with the confectioners' sugar and egg white in the food processor before kneading it. The dough rolled out well. The finger-sized rolls of dough fit nicely into the rings, but in the low-temperature oven, the dough exploded out of the rings. Some say that if the dough is too moist it will rise to excess. Maybe this is what happened, or the dough was overmixed, or I added too much cream of tartar.*

*Another time, I made a beautiful kransekake for my cousin, carefully decorated it, and placed it in the car in a protective box to travel to the southern part of Virginia. The kransekake rings were so moist and the weather so hot that by the time I arrived and opened the trunk, the top rings had sunk down into the larger bottom rings. So my cousin used the kransekake she had made as a centerpiece, and broke mine into pieces to spread around the centerpiece for people to eat. At least it still tasted good. She kept telling me that it tasted very good, and better than the beautiful one, but maybe that was to make me feel better.*

*While in Vietnam I received kransekaker in the mail from Mother. She had carefully wrapped each ring separately in plastic wrap. Then she put all of the rings in a big box and put popcorn all around each ring. All the rings traveled safely all that way. When it arrived I was so surprised, and I put the kransekake together and ate the popcorn. Of course, I had to have a party, and several of them before we finished it.*

*If you make the cake ahead of time, freeze the kransekake rings separately, unfrosted, or divide the frosted cake into two stacks and freeze. This cake is usually made in 13 or 18 separate rings, each slightly smaller than the next. The cake, after assembly, is decorated with swirls of white frosting and then with little Norwegian flags on toothpicks or pins and other symbols for the occasion, such as little presents, Christmas ornaments, or wedding symbols. Some people put a peeled apple in the center to keep it moist, especially if they are not going to serve it right away. I don't like to do that, as sometimes I have forgotten the apple and it manages to go bad. This recipe should make 18 rings, but depending on the diameter of the rings, you might have to make two or more batches of the dough.*

*I now use almond paste, but when we were children, Gudrun made her almond flour from scratch. She would blanch the almonds, and Eddie and I would remove the brown skin from each almond, one by one. Then we ground them by hand in a 12-inch curved wooden bowl with a double-bladed chopping knife. We chopped and chopped, and then Gudrun took over and chopped and ground them with the double-bladed knife until they were as fine as powder. Now there are both hand and electric grinders. However, it does not work to grind or chop the nuts into flour in a food processer. For a kransekake made with almond paste, see the next recipe.*

*This cake can be frozen and refrozen. We eat it from the bottom ring up to the top, lifting it up and pulling out a few rings from the bottom to break up and put around the kransekake for people to eat. That way it continues to serve as a lovely decoration and centerpiece.  —Irene*

**Batter**
1 pound ground almonds
2 teaspoons almond extract
4 egg whites, unbeaten
1 pound confectioners' sugar
Pinch of salt

**Frosting**
1½ cups sifted confectioners' sugar
1 egg white
1 teaspoon vinegar

Special equipment: *kransekake* forms, pastry bag

Preheat oven to 275 degrees. Combine ground almonds and almond extract in a medium bowl. A little at a time, add egg whites to almonds, blending thoroughly with a potato masher. Add confectioners' sugar and salt and blend. Transfer mixture to the top of a double boiler and cook slowly, stirring with a wooden spoon, until dough is well mixed and warmed, about 10 to 15 minutes.

It is essential to prepare the forms well so that the rings will not stick and break as you are removing them. You can spray with vegetable spray and sprinkle with farina, semolina, or Cream of Wheat to prevent the dough from sticking in the forms. I find that the batter is firm and will not pour, so I roll the batter into cylinders the width of my largest finger (or the diameter of my *kransekake* forms) and then place each ring carefully into the form. (Some people use a cookie press to put the dough into the form.) Put the ends together so that it is seamless. Place the forms on a cookie sheet and bake for about 15 minutes or until golden. Place each form upside down on a table or rack to cool completely.

While the cakes (rings) are cooling, make the frosting. Stir together confectioners' sugar, egg white, and vinegar with a spoon or whisk. If it is not stiff enough to stick to the rings in waves or scallops, add more powdered sugar. Put the frosting in a pastry tube with a small round tip or in a sturdy plastic bag with one corner snipped off. Be sure to assemble the cake while the frosting is still soft.

To assemble the *kransekake*, first spread some frosting on a platter to anchor the cake. The platter should be at least 1 inch bigger than the diameter of the largest ring. Place the largest ring on the platter and apply frosting in scallops, making sure the frosting goes over the edge of each ring and that the extra icing becomes an adhesive to hold the rings together. Place the next smaller ring on top and repeat until all forms are stacked. The scalloped frosting will hold each ring in place, but you may want to slide toothpicks between the layers to help secure the rings. Decorate with small Norwegian flags on toothpicks, marzipan fruit, tiny wrapped presents, or foil-wrapped candy, all on stickpins or toothpicks. Place an ornament on the top suitable for the occasion. Sometimes I have placed a small troll on top.

Serve cake from the bottom up, preserving its pyramid shape. Break up the large rings and arrange on the cake plate around the remainder of the *kransekake*.

# *Kransekake* Made with Almond Paste

*All the real Norwegian cooks, even in the Washington, D.C., area, make* kransekake *the way Gudrun did, and I do think they taste better, but for convenience I now often use almond paste to make this cake. If you wish to try this recipe with real almonds, you will need about 5½ cups blanched almonds, ground in small batches using an almond grinder or blender at high speed. It does not work to use a food processor. This batch yields enough dough to fill 9 or 10 forms; I find I need to make a double batch to get 18 rings. (Perhaps that is because I end up breaking some rings getting them out of the forms and have to make more!) —Irene*

**Batter**
Shortening or butter
Farina, semolina, or Cream of Wheat for dusting the pan
1 pound almond paste
1 pound confectioners' sugar, sifted
2 egg whites, unbeaten
¼ cup confectioners' sugar for kneading the dough

**Frosting**
1½ cups confectioners' sugar, sifted
1 egg white
1 teaspoon vinegar

Special equipment: *kransekake* forms, pastry bag

Preheat oven to 300 degrees. Grease the graduated forms with unsalted butter or vegetable oil, sprinkle with farina, semolina or Cream of Wheat, shake off any excess, and set aside.

Place almond paste and confectioners' sugar in a food processor and blend by pulsing a few times. Be careful not to overmix.

Add egg whites and blend in with a few more pulses of the food processor—again, not too much. You also may knead the egg white into the dough by hand.

Place the bowl containing the dough into hot water or place the dough in the top of a double boiler, with boiling water in the bottom pan. Knead or stir the dough until it is lukewarm. Turn the dough out on a board sprinkled with ¼ cup of confectioners' sugar. Let the dough rest for 10 minutes.

Knead dough for 2 to 3 minutes. If the dough is too moist, you may add a tiny bit of flour and more confectioners' sugar. But if the dough is not moist enough, cookbook author Astrid Karlsen Scott suggests adding a little more egg white. She also recommends testing first by baking a few sample small rings: if the dough is too dry, the cake will not rise and will be hard and dry.

Form the dough into long cylinders the width of a finger, either rolling by hand or putting dough through a cookie press with a large opening. Roll out portions of the dough one ring at a time and cut ends with a knife. Place the edges together to form a perfect circle inside each greased, graduated ring form.

Place the rings on a cookie sheet and bake in the center of the oven for 20 minutes, checking often, until rings are light beige. You can also lower your oven temperature to 250 degrees, as Gudrun often did.

Remove the forms from the oven and place on a table or rack to cool while still inside the ring forms. Do not remove the rings from the forms until they have cooled fully.

While waiting for the rings to cool, make the frosting by blending all ingredients well in a medium bowl. Place frosting in a pastry cone or sturdy plastic bag with one corner snipped off. Be sure to assemble the cake while the frosting is still soft.

When the rings have cooled, gently turn each ring form upside down. The cake should slide out of the ring easily. Assemble and serve the *kransekake* following the directions in the previous recipe.

# Mama's Cake

*When Gudrun called this "Mama's cake," we thought she was talking about herself. But it may have been a type of "hurry up" favorite of her own mother, Ingeborg Maurstad Thue, who was also known as an especially good cook.*

**Batter**
½ cup potato flour
½ cup cake flour
2–3 heaping teaspoons baking powder
¼ teaspoon salt
½ cup granulated sugar
1 teaspoon vanilla
½ teaspoon almond extract (may need
     more or less depending on quality)
3 eggs, beaten
4 tablespoons water

**Filling**
Strawberries
2 cups whipped cream
Rum Filling (see recipe below)

Preheat oven to 350 degrees. Grease two round cake pans. Sift together flours, baking powder, and salt. In another bowl, blend sugar, vanilla, and almond extract. Add eggs. While mixing, gradually add water and flour to egg mixture.

Pour batter into cake pans. Bake 25 minutes or until a toothpick inserted in the center comes out clean. Allow the cakes to cool. Layer cakes with sliced strawberries, whipped cream, or rum filling. Top with whipped cream.

**Rum Filling**

*This filling can be used for Mama's Cake or Bløtkake (page 154). Be sure to allow enough time, at least 1 hour, for it to cool before assembling the cake.*

> 2 cups whole milk
> 2 large eggs
> ⅔ cup sugar
> ⅓ cup flour
> 1 cup rum

Bring milk to a boil in a double boiler. As soon as it starts to boil, immediately lower heat to a gentle simmer.

In a separate bowl, beat eggs. Add sugar, flour, and ½ cup of scalded milk to eggs and blend until smooth with a whisk or electric mixer on low. Add egg mixture to simmering milk in double boiler. Stir until it bubbles up and thickens. Remove from the double boiler and let cool (30 minutes to 1 hour). When fully cooled, stir in rum. The filling should be thick. Some of the rum would soak into the baked cake.

# Orange Spice Cake

**Batter**

1 cup raisins

1 large orange, unpeeled and
    sliced thin (including rind)

8 tablespoons (1 stick) butter

1 cup sugar

2 eggs

2 cups cake flour, sifted

1 teaspoon baking powder

½ teaspoon salt

1 cup sour cream

½ teaspoon ground cloves

½ teaspoon cinnamon

Dash of vanilla extract or lemon juice

**Orange Glaze**

8 tablespoons (1 stick) butter,
    softened

1 pound confectioners' sugar

2 tablespoons orange juice

Preheat oven to 350 degrees and grease a 9 x 13-inch pan. Wash and dry raisins and chop together with orange slices in a bowl. Cream butter and sugar. Beat in eggs. Add chopped orange and raisins.

In another bowl, mix together flour, baking powder, and salt. Add sour cream. Stir in cloves, cinnamon, and vanilla or lemon juice. Add to egg mixture. Add more grated orange rind if the flavor is not sharp enough. Pour batter into prepared pan and bake for 35 minutes or until a toothpick inserted in the center comes out clean. Set cake to cool in the pan on a wire rack.

While the cake is baking, prepare the glaze. Using an electric mixer, blend softened butter, confectioners' sugar, and orange juice until smooth. Spread glaze over the baked cake. Cake should be glazed while still hot from the oven.

# Walnut Cake

8 tablespoons (1 stick) butter
2 cups sugar
1 egg, separated
2 teaspoons vanilla extract
1 teaspoon almond extract
3 cups sifted cake flour
½ teaspoon salt
½ teaspoon baking soda
1 cup milk
1 cup finely chopped walnuts
1 teaspoon cream of tartar
Confectioners' sugar
Whipped cream

Preheat oven to 325 degrees. Grease an 8-inch tart pan with removable sides or an 8-inch springform pan. Using an electric mixer, cream butter and sugar. Beat egg yolk slightly and blend into butter mixture, using the electric mixer. Blend in vanilla and almond extracts.

In another bowl, sift together flour, salt, and baking soda. Alternating, add flour mixture and milk to butter mixture. Stir in chopped walnuts.

In another bowl, thoroughly beat egg white until foamy. Add cream of tartar. Beat until stiff peaks form. Fold egg white into cake batter and pour batter into prepared pan. Bake 1 hour 15 minutes or until a toothpick inserted in the center comes out clean. Let cake cool inside its pan on a wire rack, then remove from pan, sprinkle with confectioners' sugar, and top with whipped cream.

# Cookies, Brownies, and Bars

Almond Wafers

Applesauce Oatmeal Cookies

Banana Oatmeal Cookies

Bourbon Balls

Chocolate Pinwheels

Macaroons

Coconut Macaroons with Almond Paste

Coconut Macaroons

Golden Coconut Mounds

Coconut Cookies

Gudrun's Brownies

Gudrun's Chocolate Chip Cookies

*Hjortetakk* (Norwegian Hartshorn Cookies)

*Krumkake*

Rosettes

*Moltekrem* (Cloudberry Cream)

*Goro*

Lemon Bars

Oatmeal Raisin Cookies

Orange Sugar Cookies

Peanut Butter Cookies

Puffball Cookies

*Sandbakkels* (Sand Tarts)

Spritz Cookies

Timble Cookies

Toffee Bars

*Troll Krem* (Troll Cream)

# Almond Wafers

1 egg
1 cup packed dark brown sugar
¼ cup flour
3 tablespoons unsalted butter, melted
1 teaspoon vanilla extract
1 cup slivered almonds

Preheat oven to 350 degrees and grease cookie sheets. In a large bowl, beat egg with electric mixer until thickened. Add brown sugar, flour, melted butter, and vanilla extract and combine. Stir in almonds using a wooden spoon or spatula. Drop dough by the teaspoonful onto cookie sheets and bake until edges begin to brown, about 10 minutes. Place cookies on a wire rack to cool.

# Applesauce Oatmeal Cookies

*This recipe makes about 4 dozen cookies, depending on the size you make.*

1 cup flour
1 teaspoon salt
1 teaspoon cinnamon
½ teaspoon baking powder
½ teaspoon baking soda
8 tablespoons (1 stick) unsalted butter, softened
¾ cup brown sugar
1 egg
1 teaspoon vanilla extract
1 cup applesauce
3 cups rolled oats
1 cup raisins

Preheat oven to 350 degrees and grease cookie sheets. In a small bowl, combine flour, salt, cinnamon, baking powder, and baking soda. In a large mixing bowl, use an electric mixer to cream butter and brown sugar. Beat in egg and vanilla extract. Stir in applesauce. Blend in the flour mixture, then stir in rolled oats, and finally add the raisins. Place teaspoonfuls of cookie dough on cookie sheets and bake until golden brown, about 12 to 15 minutes. Place cookies on a wire rack to cool.

# Banana Oatmeal Cookies

*Makes about 3½ dozen cookies.*

> 1½ cups flour, sifted
> 1 teaspoon salt
> ¾ teaspoon cinnamon
> ½ teaspoon baking soda
> ¼ teaspoon nutmeg
> ¾ cup shortening or 12 tablespoons (1½ sticks) butter
> 1 cup sugar
> 1 cup mashed ripe banana
> 1¾ cups rolled oats
> ½ cup chopped nuts or raisins (optional)

Preheat oven to 400 degrees and grease cookie sheets. In a medium-sized bowl, blend flour, salt, cinnamon, baking soda, and nutmeg. In a separate bowl, cream together shortening or butter and sugar using an electric mixer. Blend in mashed banana. Add the flour mixture and mix thoroughly, then stir in oats and nuts or raisins using a wooden spoon. Drop dough by teaspoonfuls onto cookie sheets, about 1½ inches apart. Bake 10 to 15 minutes or until golden brown.

# Bourbon Balls

*Gudrun served these at Christmas. They don't require baking and keep indefinitely when stored in a cool spot. They are best made one day ahead.*

> 3 cups ground vanilla wafers
> 1 cup ground walnuts or pecans
> 1 cup confectioners' sugar
> ½ cup bourbon, whiskey, rum, or blackberry brandy
> 3 tablespoons light corn syrup
> 1½ tablespoons cocoa
> Confectioners' sugar for decorating

Combine ground vanilla wafers, nuts, 1 cup confectioners' sugar, liquor, corn syrup, and cocoa and mix well. Form dough into 1-inch balls and roll in confectioners' sugar.

# Chocolate Pinwheels

*These refrigerator cookies need time to chill before baking.*

> 8 tablespoons (1 stick) unsalted butter
> ½ cup sugar
> 1 teaspoon vanilla extract
> ¼ teaspoon salt
> 1 egg yolk
> 1½ cups sifted flour
> ½ teaspoon baking powder
> 3 tablespoons heavy cream
> 1 square (1 ounce) milk or semisweet chocolate, melted

Using an electric mixer, cream butter, sugar, vanilla extract, salt, and egg yolk. In a separate bowl, combine flour and baking powder. With the mixer on low, alternate folding the heavy cream and the flour mixture into the butter mixture.

Divide the dough in half. Blend melted chocolate into one half. Refrigerate both doughs until chilled, about 10 minutes.

Roll each portion of dough into thin rectangular sheets about 6 inches by 9 inches. Place chocolate dough sheet on top of vanilla dough sheet. Starting from the short side, roll up the doughs tightly, as you would a jelly roll. Wrap dough in wax paper and chill in the refrigerator until firm, about 2 hours or overnight.

Preheat oven to 400 degrees and grease cookie sheets. Remove chilled dough from wax paper and cut into quarter-inch slices. Bake 12 minutes or until lightly browned and crisp.

# Macaroons

*Gudrun made many types of macaroons, and we liked them all. She usually made these on the small side, about 1 or 1½ inches in diameter.*

> 1 pound almond paste
> 6 egg whites, divided
> 1 cup granulated sugar
> 2 cups confectioners' sugar

Preheat the oven to 325 degrees. Use your hands or a wooden spoon to soften the almond paste, and then work in one-quarter of the egg whites until no lumps remain. Gradually add another one-fourth of the egg whites and half of the granulated sugar. When this is worked in, add half of the remaining egg whites with the balance of the granulated sugar and the confectioners' sugar. Then add the rest of the egg whites and work in until smooth. The consistency of the mixture should be such that when the macaroons are dropped they will not run.

Using a teaspoon, drop macaroons onto parchment paper. They should be the size of a quarter, with the point in the center. Remove the points by pressing them lightly with a dampened cloth. Bake for about 15 minutes or until golden but still chewy within. Allow to cool. When macaroons are cooled, wipe a wet towel on the underside of the parchment paper to loosen the cookies before removing them.

# Coconut Macaroons with Almond Paste

8 ounces almond paste

¾ cup granulated sugar

3 egg whites

⅓ cup confectioners' sugar

Pinch of salt

1⅓ cups sweetened or unsweetened flaked coconut

2 teaspoons almond extract

Preheat oven to 325 degrees and line a cookie sheet with parchment paper. Crumble almond paste into a bowl. Add granulated sugar a little at a time, mixing well. Using an electric mixer, beat in egg whites until well blended. Stir in confectioners' sugar and salt. Fold in coconut and almond extract.

Drop rounded teaspoonfuls of dough onto the paper. Bake until golden, about 15 minutes. Slide the paper off the baking sheet and onto a damp cloth or dish towel. Let stand for 2 minutes and then slide cookies off paper and onto a rack to cool. (You can also remove the cookies from the paper by using the method described in the previous recipe.)

# Coconut Macaroons

5 egg whites
2 cups confectioners' sugar
8 ounces sweetened flaked coconut (about 2¾ cups)
1 teaspoon vanilla extract
1 teaspoon almond extract

Preheat oven to 300 degrees and grease baking sheets. Using an electric mixer, whip the egg whites until stiff peaks form. Gradually add the confectioners' sugar. Stir in coconut. Add vanilla extract and almond extract. Drop dough by the teaspoonful onto baking sheets. Bake until golden outside but still soft and chewy, about 20 minutes.

# Golden Coconut Mounds

*These cookies dry out easily. Keep them in an airtight container in the refrigerator.*

2 eggs
1 cup sugar
3 cups sweetened flaked coconut
¼ cup sifted flour

Preheat oven to 350 degrees and grease baking sheets. In a large bowl, beat eggs with sugar. Fold in the coconut and flour. Drop dough by the teaspoonful onto baking sheets and bake until golden, 10 to 18 minutes. The cookies will still be soft but will firm up as they cool.

# Coconut Cookies

*These turn out even better if the dough is chilled before baking.*

8 tablespoons (1 stick) unsalted butter
½ cup granulated sugar
½ cup brown sugar
1 egg
1 teaspoon vanilla extract
½ cup flour
½ teaspoon baking powder
½ teaspoon baking soda
½ teaspoon salt
1 cup sweetened flaked coconut
1 scant cup rolled oats

Preheat oven to 350 degrees and grease baking sheets. Cream butter with white and brown sugars. Blend in egg and vanilla extract. In a separate bowl, sift flour with baking powder, baking soda, and salt. Slowly add flour mixture to butter mixture. Stir in coconut and oats. Drop dough by teaspoonfuls onto baking sheets and bake until golden brown, about 8 minutes.

# Gudrun's Brownies

*These were Gudrun's "hurry-up" dessert. She served them with vanilla or mint ice cream or freshly whipped whipping cream. These brownies were also in Eddie's chocolate cookbook, written by hand when he was about seven years old.*

8 tablespoons (1 stick) unsalted butter
2 squares (1 ounce each) of unsweetened chocolate
2 eggs, beaten
1 cup sugar
2–3 teaspoons vanilla extract, to taste
½ cup cake flour
¼ teaspoon salt
2 pinches baking powder

Preheat oven to 350 degrees. Grease and flour an 8 x 8-inch baking dish. In a double boiler, melt butter and chocolate together over low heat.

In a large bowl, beat eggs well, then gradually add sugar while beating and beat until smooth and creamy. Add vanilla extract. Add chocolate-butter mixture to egg mixture and blend.

Sift together flour, salt, and baking powder. Repeat. Add flour mixture to batter and mix thoroughly. Pour batter into prepared baking dish and bake for 25 to 30 minutes or until a toothpick inserted in the center comes out clean.

# Gudrun's Chocolate Chip Cookies

*This was one of Gudrun's signature cookies. When I was working in Vietnam for the United States Agency for International Development, she mailed these cookies to me, wrapping each one individually in waxed paper and placing them snugly inside Pringles cylinders. She then packed all the Pringles cylinders in popcorn. When I opened the box, the cookies were still crisp and fragrant and not one was broken after the long journey.*

*Both Eddie and I watched her make these and wrote down the recipe for the numerous people who requested it. But everyone said their cookies just didn't taste the same as Gudrun's. Had she left some ingredient out? I have made her chocolate chip cookies countless times, in single, double, and triple batches, but my cookies don't taste the same as hers either. The cookies are crisp, and are supposed to stay crisp.*

*These are usually gone before the end of the day, so I like to make a double batch. This recipe makes about 3 dozen cookies.  —Irene*

1 cup cake flour

2 teaspoons baking powder

½ teaspoon salt

8 tablespoons (1 stick) unsalted butter, room temperature

½ cup granulated sugar

½ cup light or dark brown sugar

1 egg, room temperature

2 teaspoons vanilla extract

1 teaspoon almond extract

½ teaspoon baking soda dissolved in ½ teaspoon water

1½ cups (one 12-ounce bag) semisweet or milk chocolate chips

Preheat oven to 350 degrees and grease a baking sheet. Sift the flour with baking powder and salt and set aside. Cream butter and sugars. Add egg, flour mixture, vanilla extract, almond extract, and baking soda dissolved in water to creamed butter and sugar and combine. Stir in chocolate chips. Drop teaspoonfuls of dough onto the baking sheet about 2 inches apart. (I usually press the tops down gently with a fork before putting them in the oven.) Bake until golden brown, about 10 to 12 minutes. Let cookies cool for 5 to 10 minutes before removing from baking sheet and placing them on a wire rack.

## *Hjortetakk* (Norwegian Hartshorn Cookies)

*Hjortetakksalt, or hartshorn salt, a leavening agent, at one time was made from deer antlers, according to Astrid Karlsen Scott's* Ekte Norsk Mat: Authentic Norwegian Cooking. *Now chemically produced, it is available in Scandinavian delicatessens and at drugstores, where it may be labeled ammonium carbonate, aqua ammoniae, or hartshorn salt. Before baking powder was readily available, Scott says, hartshorn salt helped provide a characteristic crispness and delicate texture to Norwegian cookies and crackers.*

*These cookies are faster and more fun to make with a friend. One person rolls the pencil-sized cylinders and forms them into wreaths while the other fries them. Eddie and I used to sit at the kitchen table, rolling and forming cookies one by one, before Gudrun slipped them into the hot oil and watched them carefully.*

*This dough requires overnight refrigeration before frying. Note: If you choose to use ground almonds, reduce the initial flour by 1 cup. Cover and refrigerate dough overnight.*
—*Irene*

> 5 cups sifted flour, divided
> Pinch of salt
> 1 teaspoon *hjortetakksalt* or 1 teaspoon baking powder
> 8 egg yolks, room temperature
> 2 cups sugar
> ½ pint whipping cream (1 cup, whipped)
> ¼ pound (1 stick) unsalted butter, melted and cooled
> Grated zest of 1 lemon
> 2–3 teaspoons ground cardamom, to taste
> 1 cup finely ground almonds (optional)
> Lard or other fat or oil for deep-frying

Special equipment: Gudrun deep-fried these one or two at a time in a deep pan on top of the stove, but I use a Fry Baby or Fry Daddy with vegetable oil and heat the oil to 375 degrees instead of 400.

Sift together 4 cups of flour, salt, and *hjortetakksalt* or baking powder and set aside. Beat egg yolks with electric beater until well mixed. Beat in the sugar, a little at a time. Fold in whipped cream, then melted butter. Add lemon zest and cardamom. A little at a time, blend in flour mixture. Sift remaining cup of flour into batter and blend using the electric mixer. Stir in ground almonds if desired. Refrigerate dough overnight.

Heat the fat to 400 degrees. If the dough is difficult to work with after being refrigerated, you may need to add additional flour. Flour hands and sprinkle flour on a clean countertop. Roll 1½- to 2-inch balls of dough into pencil-thick lengths about 6 inches long, trimming if necessary. Form small wreaths about 1 inch in diameter by making a ring and overlapping ends. With a sharp knife, make two or three incisions on the outside of each ring.

Deep-fry two or three cookies at a time (no more than three) in the hot lard or oil until golden. Remove them with a slotted spoon and set them on a paper towel first to drain the grease, and then on a baking rack to cool. Store in an airtight container.

# Krumkake

Toward the end of World War II, Gudrun received a big package from her sister Ingeborg. It had traveled thousands of miles, from a Nazi-occupied nation across the battlefield of the Atlantic Ocean to the American Midwest. Out on our back porch on Riverside Drive, Gudrun opened the package. Inside was the biggest smoked salmon she had ever seen. And inside the smoked salmon, all tied together and wrapped in a Norwegian newspaper, was a cast-iron Jøtul krumkake iron. Whenever she made krumkake, she always told the story of the iron's perilous journey, safeguarded within the impenetrable fortification of a giant smoked salmon.

The dough requires chilling time in the refrigerator. If it chills overnight, let it warm at room temperature long enough to be pliable, but still cold enough to let the pattern from the krumkake iron show up well. If you are making them right away, chill for at least an hour in the refrigerator before baking.

A krumkake rolling cone is a wooden cone the size and shape of an ice cream sugar cone, but with a handle. Some people use a wooden dowl or cylinder about 6 inches long. Gudrun had two sizes of cones, a standard size and a larger one. (We usually use the standard size.)

Serve these crisp krumkaker plain or with cloudberry cream (moltekrem; see page 193), whipped cream, and fresh or frozen strawberries or blueberries. The cookies should stay crisp, so I serve the bowl of whipped cream (or Cool Whip) and the bowl of sliced strawberries separately for guest to serve themselves. This recipe makes about 3 dozen krumkaker and can be doubled. Often I tell people to eat it by nibbling around the edges where the cookie is rolled up. Otherwise, the cookie will crumble completely with the first bite—causing a surprised look on the face of the krumkake eater! —Irene

> ½ pound (2 sticks) unsalted butter
> 4 eggs
> 1 cup sugar
> 2 cups flour, sifted
> ¼ teaspoon baking powder
> 1 tablespoon ground cardamom, or more to taste

1 teaspoon almond extract

1 teaspoon vanilla extract

¼ teaspoon salt

Special equipment: cast-iron or electric *krumkake* iron, rolling cone

Melt butter and let cool to room temperature. In a separate bowl, beat eggs with an electric mixer until thick. While beating, gradually add sugar, 1 tablespoon at a time.

Sift baking powder into sifted flour. Alternating, add butter and flour to egg mixture a little at a time, beating between additions. Add cardamom, almond extract, vanilla extract, and salt. Mix well with electric mixer. Cover and refrigerate dough until very cold and solid, at least 1 hour or as long as overnight.

Wipe dry the patterned side of the *krumkake* iron with a paper towel. There is no need to grease the iron, as there is so much butter in the dough. Set an electric *krumkake* iron to medium-low, or heat both sides of a cast-iron *krumkake* iron. When a drop of water placed on the iron bubbles dry, the iron is ready. Press a spoonful of dough about the size of a big walnut onto the center of the iron; close the iron and bake for approximately 45 seconds.

If using a cast-iron *krumkake* iron, turn it over and bake on the other side for another 45 seconds, until cookie is light golden on each side. You may need to open the iron to check if the cookie is done, but that runs the risk of disturbing the pattern. You may also watch for steam coming from the iron to know when each side is done. (If you are using the electric iron, you do not have to turn it over, as the iron cooks both sides of the cookie.) Remove cookie with a metal spatula and place on waxed paper.

Immediately, while the cookie is still very hot, roll it up on a rolling cone. Let it cool on the cone until crisp. (You may also form them into a cup by pressing hot *krumkake* directly from the iron into a coffee cup.) When the cookie has firmed, gently slide it off the cone and set aside on a plate or other container to finish cooling. The *krumkaker* can be kept in the freezer. In the humid summers of Wisconsin it was difficult to keep them crisp when they were out in the air, so Gudrun kept them in the refrigerator or freezer or at least in an airtight container.

# Rosettes

*This recipe is adapted from one in one of Gudrun's older cookbooks. Making rosettes requires a special rosette iron, available from specialty cookware shops. The rosette iron includes an iron stick and two or three shaped forms, such as a wheel, star, and butterfly. This recipe makes about 30 rosette cookies; I usually double or triple it when cooking for Christmas.* —Irene

3 eggs
1 cup whole milk
2 tablespoons sugar
1½ cups flour
2 tablespoons melted butter
Shortening or hot vegetable oil for frying
Confectioners' sugar, sifted

Special equipment: Rosette iron (stick and forms); I use an electric Fry Baby or Fry Daddy, but you also can use a heavy saucepan on top of the stove

Whisk the eggs, milk, and sugar lightly together with a wire whisk. Sift the flour over the egg mixture and fold gently until the ingredients are just combined. Add the melted butter and mix again. Refrigerate the batter for 30 minutes.

Heat the shortening or oil to 350 degrees. Screw the rosette form onto the stick and heat the rosette iron in the fat until hot. Dip the iron into the batter. The batter should just reach the top of the iron but not go over it. Dip the iron with batter sticking to it into the hot fat until cookie is nicely browned. Deep fry until cookie is just stiff, about 1 minute. Remove the rosette with a fork and drain on paper towels. Continue with remaining batter.

Sprinkle rosettes with sifted confectioners' sugar. Some people do this just before serving. To store, stack layers of the rosettes between sheets of waxed paper in an airtight container. These will keep at room temperature for about 3 months.

# *Moltekrem* (Cloudberry Cream)

*Molter (cloudberries) resemble raspberries in their appearance, but the flavor is unique. These berries grow in the mountain marshland. Gudrun often talked about going into the mountains for her mother to look for molter, which are rich in vitamin C. The berries are used for jam and various desserts after the seeds have been removed with a sieve. Cloudberry jam is available in Scandinavian specialty stores.*

> 1½ cups whipping cream
> 4 tablespoons confectioners' sugar
> 1 teaspoon vanilla extract or vanilla sugar
> ½ cup *molte* (cloudberry) jam

Combine whipping cream, confectioners' sugar, and vanilla extract or vanilla sugar in a medium-sized bowl. Using an electric mixer, whip the cream until soft peaks form. Fold in the cloudberry jam.

# Goro

Goro *is short for* gode råd, *which means "good advice." These crisp, cardamom-scented Christmas treats are somewhere between a cookie, a cracker, and a waffle. The goro iron is similar to a krumkake iron, but with a different shape. This recipe makes about 12 dozen small, thin goro (depending on the type of iron—usually 48 full-sized pieces each cut into 3 goro, or 36 pieces each cut into 4 goro). Immediately after removing the cookies from the goro iron, while the cookie is warm, use a sharp knife to cut the large cookie into 3 or 4 separate cookies, using the marks made by the iron. The dough will need to be refrigerated for 24 hours before baking, and the baked cookies can be frozen. My cousin Bjorg has sent me every type of Norwegian cookie, including* goro *and* kransekake, *through the postal system.*
*—Irene*

3 egg yolks
½ cup sugar
1 cup whipping cream
1 tablespoon cognac
1 teaspoon ground cardamom
1 teaspoon vanilla extract
5 cups flour, divided
1 pound (4 sticks) butter

Special equipment: *goro* iron, cardboard or paper template the same size as iron for cutting dough, pastry cutter

Beat the egg yolks with an electric mixer. Add the sugar and continue beating until mixture is lemon-colored. In a separate bowl, whip the cream, then stir whipped cream into egg mixture. Add the cognac, cardamom, and vanilla extract and combine. A little at a time, sift 2½ cups flour into the egg mixture and beat to combine.

Sprinkle the remaining flour on a pastry board or bread board and turn dough onto it. Roll just enough additional flour into the dough so that the dough can be rolled out as you would for cookies. When dough has been rolled out, spread the butter in thin layers across the dough. Fold the dough over in half and roll out again. Spread again with remaining butter and roll the dough over again. Roll up the dough in a cylinder shape and chill for 24 hours in the refrigerator.

Take dough out of the refrigerator and roll it out thin. Take a small piece of the dough about 4 inches in diameter, and roll it out about ⅛-inch thick, slightly thicker than *krumkake*. Make a cardboard or paper template the size of the *goro* iron. Heat the iron on the stovetop until a drop of water sizzles on its surface.

Trace and cut cookies the size of the pattern with a pastry cutter. Then place the cookie on the *goro* iron and bake until the cookie is light golden brown. (As the cookie is baking, some of the butter will leak out; simply keep wiping it off the stove.) Turn the iron over after 1 minute and bake the other side. Remove cookie from the *goro* iron with a metal spatula and place the cookie on a cutting board. Cut off any frayed edges. Cut apart with the pastry cutter or knife while the cookies are still hot. Cool completely. Store in an airtight container between layers of waxed paper. Cookies can be frozen for up to three months.

# Lemon Bars

**Crust**
8 tablespoons (1 stick) unsalted butter, softened
1 cup flour
¼ cup confectioners' sugar

**Filling**
2 eggs
1 cup granulated sugar
2 tablespoons flour
2 tablespoons lemon juice
Zest of 1 lemon
¼ teaspoon baking powder
Confectioners' sugar for dusting

Preheat oven to 350 degrees. To make the crust, combine butter, flour, and confectioners' sugar in a medium-sized bowl. Pat dough into bottom of an 8 x 8-inch pan. Bake 15 minutes and remove from oven.

While crust is baking, beat eggs with an electric mixer, then add sugar and beat until thickened. Add flour, lemon juice and zest, and baking powder. Pour mixture over partially baked crust and return to oven for another 25 minutes. Sprinkle with confectioners' sugar while still warm.

# Oatmeal Raisin Cookies

*Gudrun made many types of oatmeal cookies, and this one is a favorite. Moist, tangy, and chewy, these cookies are good for dunking and keep well. This recipe makes 2 to 3 dozen cookies, depending on the size you prefer.*

> 12 tablespoons (1½ sticks) unsalted
>    butter, room temperature
> 1 cup sugar
> 1 egg, beaten
> ¼ cup molasses
> 1½ cups flour
> 1 teaspoon baking soda
> 1 teaspoon ground ginger
> 1 teaspoon cinnamon
> ¼ teaspoon salt
> 1 cup quick-cooking oats
> ⅔ cup raisins

Preheat oven to 325 degrees and grease cookie sheets. Cream butter and sugar; add egg and molasses and blend or beat with electric mixer.

In a separate bowl, sift together flour, baking soda, ground ginger, cinnamon, and salt. Beat into sugar and butter mixture. Stir in oats and raisins. Drop by teaspoonfuls onto cookie sheets. Use a fork dipped in hot water to flatten dough on cookie sheets. Bake 10 to 12 minutes or until golden brown.

# Orange Sugar Cookies

*The dough for these cookies needs to chill for 1 hour. Makes 2 dozen cookies.*

2 cups sifted flour
1½ teaspoons baking powder
¼ teaspoon salt
⅔ cup shortening
¾ cup sugar
1 egg
½ teaspoon vanilla extract
Grated zest of 1 orange
4 teaspoons milk
Granulated sugar for sprinkling

Sift together sifted flour, baking powder, and salt, and set aside. In a large bowl, cream shortening and sugar thoroughly with an electric mixer. Add egg and beat until mixture is light and fluffy. Add vanilla extract and orange zest; combine thoroughly. Stir flour mixture into shortening mixture along with milk. (You can use the electric mixer for this, or you can stir by hand as Gudrun did.) Divide the dough in half and chill 1 hour, until dough is easy to handle.

Preheat oven to 375 degrees and grease a cookie sheet. Keep one half of the dough chilled until you're ready to roll it. Roll the other half ⅛-inch thick. Cut into shapes with a cookie cutter and place on greased cookie sheet. Sprinkle cookies lightly with sugar and bake for 12 minutes or until golden.

# Peanut Butter Cookies

*These cookies were a favorite of ours. They were crisp and about 1 inch in diameter. We ate them with lots of cold milk. This recipe makes about 2 to 3 dozen cookies depending on the size. Gudrun always scored the top with a fork, pressing down lightly while the cookie was warm from the oven. You can also score them before baking, but the pattern will not be as clear.*

    8 tablespoons (1 stick) unsalted butter
    ½ cup brown sugar
    ½ cup granulated sugar
    1 cup cake flour
    1 egg
    ½ cup peanut butter
    1 tablespoon grated orange zest
    1 teaspoon vanilla extract
    1 teaspoon cinnamon
    ½ teaspoon baking soda mixed with 1 teaspoon water
    Pinch of apple pie spice

Preheat oven to 325 degrees and grease cookie sheets. Using an electric mixer, cream butter and sugars. Add flour, egg, peanut butter, orange zest, vanilla extract, cinnamon, baking soda mixture, and apple pie spice, and mix well, forming a dough. Using teaspoons, drop dough onto cookie sheets, ½ teaspoon at a time. Crisscross a fork dipped in cold water over each cookie. Bake 15 to 20 minutes or until golden brown. Let cookies cool for 1 to 2 minutes before removing from cookie sheet and placing on a wire rack.

# Puffball Cookies

*This fun recipe makes about 3 dozen cookies, depending on size.*

8 tablespoons (1 stick) unsalted butter, softened
1 cup flour, sifted
¾ cup ground or finely chopped nuts
1 tablespoon granulated sugar
1 tablespoon water
1 teaspoon vanilla extract
Confectioners' sugar for dusting

Preheat oven to 350 degrees and grease a cookie sheet. Blend all ingredients except confectioners' sugar with an electric mixer, then use your hands to roll the dough into 1-inch balls. Place on cookie sheet and bake for 15 to 20 minutes, until golden brown. Remove cookies from oven and immediately roll them in confectioners' sugar while still hot.

# *Sandbakkels* (Sand Tarts)

*These lovely, crisp little cookies taste of butter and fresh almond and are particularly good at Christmastime. Sandbakkel tins are small, fluted, tins, usually round, but also available in rectangle and other shapes, similar to a miniature tart tin.*

> Farina or Cream of Wheat for dusting tins
> ¼ pound (1 stick) unsalted butter or shortening
> 1 cup sugar
> 1 egg
> 1 cup finely ground almonds
> 2½ cups flour

Special equipment: *sandbakkel* tins

Preheat oven to 375 degrees. Grease the *sandbakkel* tins with butter or cooking spray and sprinkle with farina or Cream of Wheat.

Using an electric mixer, cream butter or shortening. Add sugar and cream well. Blend in egg and ground almonds. Add flour and combine with a wooden spoon to make a stiff dough.

To make the cookies, pinch off a small ball of dough and place it in the center of each *sandbakkel* tin. With your thumb, press dough evenly into the bottom and sides of the tin, spreading thinly (about ⅛-inch thick), but be careful not to make them too thin or they will break when turned out of the tins after baking.

Place filled tins on a cookie sheet. Bake until cookies are pale golden-tan, about 15 to 20 minutes. (Check at 10 minutes and watch closely so the cookies don't get too brown.) Remove the cookie sheet from the oven and let tins cool for a few minutes, then carefully turn tins upside down over the cookie sheet so cookies slide out easily.

# Spritz Cookies

*At Christmastime, Gudrun would sometimes divide the dough for these cookies into three parts, coloring one part red, one green, and leaving the rest naturally golden. Then she would put a tiny piece of maraschino cherry in the middle of each cookie. This dough should be chilled for 30 minutes before baking.*

½ pound (2 sticks) unsalted butter, room temperature
1½ cups confectioners' sugar
3 egg yolks, beaten
2½ cups flour
½ teaspoon baking powder
¼ teaspoon salt
1–2 teaspoons vanilla extract, to taste
¼–½ teaspoon almond extract, to taste

Special equipment: cookie press

Cream butter and confectioners' sugar with an electric mixer. Add beaten egg yolks to butter and sugar and combine thoroughly. In a separate bowl, sift flour with baking powder and salt and add slowly, with mixer running, to butter mixture. Add vanilla extract and almond extract.

Place the dough in a cookie press and push the cookies out onto ungreased cookie sheets. You can use various designs; Gudrun usually used the star design. Place cookie sheets in the refrigerator for 30 minutes before baking to allow dough to chill. (This will help the cookies hold their shapes.)

Preheat oven to 350 degrees. Bake cookies for 15 to 20 minutes or until golden. Some people bake for about 10 minutes at 400 degrees. Whatever you do, as always, use love and consideration—which in this case means to watch closely while baking.

# Timble Cookies

*Gudrun called these Timble Cookies, but I believe the name was really "thimble," for the small thimble that she sometimes used to make the well in the middle for holding the melted chocolate. This recipe is adapted from one she wrote in her own handwriting and from my notes after watching her bake these delicious treats.  —Irene*

12 tablespoons (1½ sticks) butter, room temperature
1 cup brown sugar
1 egg, separated
1 teaspoon vanilla
1½ cups flour, sifted
½ teaspoon salt
1 cup finely chopped pecans or walnuts, optional
⅔ cup chocolate chips, melted

Cream the butter and brown sugar. Beat in the egg yolk with an electric hand mixer. (Reserve the egg white.) Beat in the vanilla. Stir in the sifted flour and salt. Mix thoroughly and then roll into a large ball. (You may want to chill the dough briefly for easier handling.)

Preheat oven to 350 degrees and lightly grease a baking sheet. Pinch off pieces of dough and roll them into about 1-inch balls. In a small bowl, lightly beat the egg white. Roll each ball in the egg white and then roll in chopped nuts. Place the balls on prepared baking sheet.

Bake cookies for 5 minutes and then remove from the oven. Make a well in the center of each cookie by pushing a small thimble (or your thumb) into the dough. (Do not make a hole all the way through to the cookie sheet.) Return the cookie sheet to the oven. Bake cookies 12 minutes longer.

Remove cookies from oven and fill each indentation or hole with melted chocolate.

# Toffee Bars

*These rich bars are one of our favorites.*

½ pound (2 sticks) unsalted butter, softened
1 cup brown sugar
1 egg yolk
1 teaspoon vanilla extract
2 cups flour
Pinch of salt
6 full-size milk chocolate candy bars, such as Hershey's

Preheat oven to 375 degrees and grease a 13 x 9-inch pan. In a large bowl, cream butter and brown sugar. Add egg yolk and vanilla extract and combine. Stir in flour and salt. Pour batter into prepared pan and bake for 12 to 15 minutes. While cookies are baking, cut chocolate bars into 1-inch or 2-inch squares. Remove cookies from oven and immediately lay chocolate pieces on top to melt.

# *Troll Krem* (Troll Cream)

*This light egg-white-based dish is served in a bowl with cookies. The egg whites are not cooked, so do not use this recipe if you are not certain of the safety of your eggs. You may also substitute 2 cups lingonberry jam for the fresh lingonberries. If using jam, omit the ¾ cup sugar.*

> 2 cups fresh lingonberries, blueberries, currants, or cranberries
> ¾ cup sugar
> 3 egg whites
> 3 tablespoons sugar
> 1¼ tablespoons lemon juice

Combine berries with ¾ cup sugar, stirring with a wooden spoon until the sugar is completely dissolved. In a separate bowl, beat the egg whites until they form stiff peaks. Stir in 3 tablespoons sugar and lemon juice and continue beating until light and fluffy. Gently fold in the berries that have been mixed with sugar. Serve in a bowl with a side of cookies.

# Pies

# Graham Cracker Crust

*This is an easy, tasty graham cracker crust that melts in your mouth. You can use it for all of the recipes calling for a graham cracker crust. Eddie and I would roll over the graham crackers with a rolling pin to crush them fine, eating a few of the crackers as we went along.  —Irene*

> 1½ cups crushed graham crackers (about 16–22 crackers,
>      crushed with rolling pin)
> 8 tablespoons (1 stick) unsalted butter, softened
> ¼ cup confectioners' sugar
> 1 teaspoon vanilla extract

Mix all ingredients thoroughly. Press mixture evenly into a 9-inch pie plate and chill in the refrigerator for at least 1 hour.

# Pie Crust

*Minimize your handling of the dough in order to maximize the tenderness and flakiness of this crust. This basic recipe makes enough for two 9-inch crusts.*

> 2 cups flour
> 1 teaspoon salt
> ⅔ cup lard
> ¼ cup water

Combine flour and salt. Using a pastry blender or two knives, cut in lard until mixture resembles coarse meal. Add water all at once and blend. Form dough into two balls. Roll out one ball for bottom crust and press into a 9-inch pie plate. Roll out the other ball, cut into half-inch strips, and set aside for lattice top. Or, if making a two-crust pie, roll out an additional full crust.

# Apple Pie

*Gudrun's favorite fruit was apples. When she went to the hospital in Madison to get her gall bladder removed, she asked our father to bring her a bag of apples—and she ate the entire bag the night before the surgery. She made applesauce, apple cake, red cinnamon apple rings with pork, pickled crab apples from the tree in our yard, and apple pie from the many kinds of fresh apples that grew on the trees in our field.*

½ cup granulated sugar
1 tablespoon flour
½ teaspoon cinnamon
Pinch of salt
4 or 5 large, crisp, juicy apples,
    sliced and pared (about 6 cups)
1 Pie Crust recipe (see page 207),
    one crust pressed into pie plate,
    second crust reserved for lattice top
¾ cup brown sugar
½ cup flour
4 tablespoons (½ stick) unsalted butter

Preheat oven to 425 degrees. Blend together granulated sugar, 1 tablespoon flour, cinnamon, and salt. Toss lightly with apples and then spoon apples into pie shell. In another bowl, combine brown sugar, ½ cup flour, and butter. Sprinkle over pie filling.

Form second half of Pie Crust recipe into a lattice top and lay over pie filling. Press together edges around the pie to make it look pretty. Bake for 35 to 40 minutes or until crust is golden brown and apple juice is bubbling. Watch closely so the crust does not get too brown (you may want to reduce the oven temperature to 350 degrees while the pie is baking).

# Apple Tart

*Serve this tart with vanilla ice cream or freshly whipped cream.*

### Crust
½ stick (4 tablespoons) unsalted butter
12–16 graham crackers, crushed with a rolling pin
1 teaspoon vanilla extract

### Filling
4 tart, crisp apples
½ cup sugar, or to taste
3 eggs, separated
1 tablespoon sugar
Pinch of salt
½ cup cream or condensed milk
1 teaspoon grated lemon zest
1 teaspoon lemon juice
1 cup applesauce

To make the crust, melt butter, stir in crushed graham crackers, add vanilla extract, and stir to combine. Pat mixture into a greased 9-inch tart pan or pie pan, saving some of the mixture to sprinkle on top of tart. Chill in refrigerator.

While crust chills, make the filling. Preheat oven to 350 degrees. Peel and slice apples, place in a saucepan, and cover with water to prevent browning until ready to add them to the tart. To the saucepan add sugar to taste depending on sweetness of apples (about ½ cup). Simmer for 10 minutes. In a separate bowl, beat the egg whites, sugar, and salt together and set aside. In another bowl, beat the egg yolks. Add cream or condensed milk to yolks and blend. Blend in lemon zest and juice. Drain the apples and add them with the applesauce to the egg yolk mixture. Fold in beaten egg white mixture and pour into crust. Top with reserved graham cracker mix. Bake for 60 minutes or until golden brown.

# Cheesecake

**Crust**

⅓ cup (⅔ stick) unsalted butter

16 graham crackers, crushed
    with rolling pin

½ cup confectioners' sugar

1 teaspoon vanilla extract

**Topping**

1 can (1 pound, 6 ounces)
    cherry pie filling

¼ teaspoon almond extract

2 tablespoons sugar (optional)

**Filling**

2 eggs, separated

½ cup sugar

1 tablespoon flour

½ cup sour cream

1 package (8 ounces)
    cream cheese

1 teaspoon vanilla extract

Preheat oven to 325 degrees. Make the crust and topping: Melt ⅓ cup butter and mix in graham cracker crumbs, confectioners' sugar, and vanilla extract. Press into a 9-inch pie pan, saving some to sprinkle on top of cheesecake, and set aside. In another bowl, mix together cherry pie filling with almond extract. If the cherry topping is very tart, you may want to add 2 tablespoons sugar. We like fruit tart.

Make the filling: Using an electric mixer, beat egg whites until stiff peaks form. In a separate bowl, beat egg yolks until thick, gradually adding sugar and flour. Thoroughly blend in sour cream. Gradually add cream cheese and vanilla extract and combine thoroughly. Fold beaten egg whites into egg yolk mixture. Pour filling over graham cracker crust and bake about 45 minutes or until firm to touch. Remove and let cheesecake cool.

When cheesecake is cool, spoon cherry topping over cake. Sprinkle a little graham cracker mix around the edge of the cheesecake before serving.

# Chocolate Chiffon Pie

*Chocolate chiffon pie served with freshly whipped cream was a family favorite (and one that had a special place in Eddie's chocolate cookbook). We were always happy to see this one in the refrigerator, and it never lasted very long. Begin preparing this pie at least 4 hours in advance to allow enough chilling time. This recipe makes 8 generous slices. Use a 9-inch deep-dish pie plate.*

*Note: This recipe includes uncooked eggs, so use with caution when cooking for elderly or chronically ill persons. We gathered eggs from our own chickens; today's cooks need to know about the risk of salmonella in industrially produced eggs.*

1 envelope (.25 ounce)
 unflavored gelatin
¼ cup cold water
½ cup boiling water
2 squares (1 ounce each)
 semisweet chocolate
4 eggs, separated

1 cup sugar, divided
2 teaspoons vanilla extract
½ teaspoon cream of tartar
¼ teaspoon salt
1 Graham Cracker Crust (see page 207),
 pressed into a 9-inch pie plate
Whipped cream

Dissolve gelatin in ¼ cup cold water and set aside. Bring ½ cup water to a boil over a double boiler and add chocolate to melt. In another bowl, beat egg yolks. Gradually add ½ cup of the sugar to egg yolks, then add melted chocolate and gelatin dissolved in water to egg yolk mixture and stir to combine. Let stand and cool until it reaches custard consistency—soft, not stiff. Stir in vanilla.

Beat egg whites with an electric mixer, adding cream of tartar and salt just before the egg whites reach soft-peak stage. Gradually add remaining ½ cup sugar, beating until stiff peaks form. Fold egg white mixture into chocolate custard mixture. Pour into graham cracker crust and refrigerate until firm, 4 to 5 hours. Keep refrigerated until ready to serve. Decorate with a little whipped cream if desired.

# Chocolate Mallow Pie

*Allow adequate time for the pie to chill and set.*

> 5 full-size chocolate bars with almonds, such as Hershey's
> 20 large marshmallows
> ½ cup milk
> 1 pint whipping cream
> 1 Graham Cracker Crust (see page 207), pressed
>     into an 8-inch springform or 9-inch square pan

Over a double boiler, melt together chocolate bars, marshmallows, and milk. Set aside to cool slightly. In a separate bowl, whip whipping cream until firm peaks form, and then fold the whipped cream into chocolate mixture. Pour mixture into crust and refrigerate until firm.

# Custard Pie

> 4 eggs
> ½ cup sugar
> 1 teaspoon vanilla extract
> ¼ teaspoon salt
> 1½ cups half-and-half
> 1 cup milk, scalded
> 1 Pie Crust recipe (see page 207), bottom
>     crust only, pressed into 9-inch pie plate
> Pinch of nutmeg

Preheat oven to 400 degrees. In a large bowl, lightly beat eggs with an electric mixer. Gradually add sugar, then add vanilla extract and salt. While beating, gradually add half-and-half and scalded milk. Pour filling into unbaked pie crust and sprinkle with nutmeg. Bake for 25 to 30 minutes, until a knife inserted in the center comes out clean. Place pie on a rack to cool.

# Grasshopper Pie

*Begin this recipe several hours in advance or the day before to allow time to freeze the pie.*

### Chocolate Cookie Crust
2 tablespoons unsalted butter, melted
14 Oreos or other chocolate sandwich cookie, crushed

### Filling
24 large marshmallows
½ cup milk
1 cup whipping cream
4 tablespoons green crème de menthe
2 tablespoons white crème de cacao
Flaked chocolate for garnish

To make the crust, combine butter and crushed cookies in a large bowl. Press mixture into an 8-inch pie plate.

To make the filling, melt marshmallows in milk over a double boiler, stirring constantly, and set aside. While the marshmallow mixture cools, whip whipping cream to firm peaks.

Stir crème de menthe and crème de cacao into cooled marshmallow mixture, then fold in whipped cream and pour all into pie shell. Freeze for 4 to 5 hours. Serve frozen, with flaked chocolate for garnish.

# Gala Grasshopper Pie

*This is an even richer version of the grasshopper pie, made firmer with the addition of gelatin. Allow a few hours for the pie to chill.*

> 1 envelope (.25 ounce) unflavored gelatin
> ½ cup sugar, divided
> ⅛ teaspoon salt
> ½ cup cold water
> 3 eggs, separated
> ¼ cup green crème de menthe
> ¼ cup white crème de cacao
> 1 cup heavy cream, whipped
> Purchased chocolate crumb shell or
>     one Chocolate Cookie Crust (see page 213)
>     pressed into an 8-inch pie plate

Combine gelatin, ¼ cup sugar, and salt in a saucepan or metal bowl that can go over a double boiler. Add water and egg yolks, one at a time, stirring to blend well. Place bowl or saucepan over boiling water in a double boiler, stirring, until gelatin is dissolved and mixture thickens slightly, about 5 minutes. Remove bowl or pan from double boiler and let cool for about 10 minutes. Stir in crème de menthe and crème de cacao. Chill, stirring occasionally, until mixture is the consistency of stiff beaten egg white.

When gelatin mixture has chilled, beat egg whites until stiff peaks form. While beating, gradually add remaining ¼ cup sugar to egg whites and beat until very stiff. Fold in gelatin mixture, then fold in whipped cream. Turn filling into chocolate crumb shell and chill 4 to 5 hours.

# Lemon Angel Pie

*Gudrun served this layered creation of meringue crust, lemon filling, and whipped cream topping for special occasions like Easter and birthdays, a tradition Eddie carried on as long as he was able. When he made this pie for his granddaughter's first birthday, Addie looked over the heavenly creation and then bobbed down, face-first, into the whipped cream.*

*Begin this pie the day before serving—ideally, it should set in the refrigerator for 24 hours. If you like a lot of whipped cream, use 2 pints instead of 1 for the topping.*

**Crust**
4 egg whites
½ teaspoon cream of tartar or ¼ teaspoon baking powder
Pinch of salt
1 cup granulated sugar, divided
2 teaspoons vanilla extract
1–2 teaspoons almond extract, to taste

**Filling**
4 egg yolks
½ cup granulated sugar
Zest and juice of 2 large lemons (½ cup juice)

**Topping**
1 pint heavy whipping cream
2 tablespoons confectioners' sugar
2 teaspoons vanilla extract
Maraschino cherry

Preheat oven to 275 degrees and grease a 9-inch pie plate. To make the meringue crust, beat 4 egg whites with an electric mixer until foamy, then add cream of tartar or baking powder and salt. Beat until stiff peaks form. Add sugar 1 tablespoon at a time, beating as you go so that meringue doesn't get sandy and sugary, until all the sugar has been added. Add vanilla and almond extracts and pour egg white mixture into pie plate. Bake about 1 hour, or until meringue crust is golden brown and the edges have begun to pull away from the pan. Be careful not to overcook—I like to start checking the crust after 40 minutes just to be sure. The crust may puff up considerably but will sink a bit when you take it out of the oven. Allow the crust to cool completely before covering with filling. (You can use less sugar if you don't like it so sweet.)

As the crust cools, make the lemon filling. In a saucepan over a double boiler, beat egg yolks with an electric mixer, then gradually add granulated sugar. Add grated lemon zest and juice. Cook, stirring, until mixture resembles custard. Do not overcook, as it will start turning brownish. Remove filling from stove and cool.

To make the whipped cream topping, beat whipping cream, confectioners' sugar, and vanilla extract until stiff peaks form. Do not overbeat.

Spread a little whipped cream topping over the meringue crust. Add 3 to 4 large tablespoons of whipped cream (or more, if you like a lighter filling) to the lemon filling and mix well gently with a wooden spoon or spatula. Spoon the lemon filling over the meringue crust, then top with remaining whipped cream. Chill overnight or up to 24 hours. Place a maraschino cherry in the center of the pie before serving.

# Lemon Chiffon Pie

*Start this pie several hours ahead to allow it to cool and set.*

> 1 Graham Cracker Crust (see page 207),
>   pressed into a 9-inch pie plate
> 4 eggs, separated
> 1 cup sugar, divided
> ½ teaspoon salt
> ½ cup lemon juice
> Grated zest of 1 lemon
> ½ cup boiling water
> 1 envelope (.25 ounce) unflavored gelatin
>   dissolved in ¼ cup cold water

Using an electric mixer, beat egg whites with ½ cup sugar and ½ teaspoon salt until stiff peaks form. Set aside.

Beat egg yolks with remaining ½ cup sugar, and then add lemon juice and zest.

Place ½ cup boiling water over a double boiler; add egg yolk mixture and dissolved gelatin. Cook, while stirring, until mixture is thick and lemon-colored. Remove from heat and cool about 15 minutes, just to room temperature (you don't want the gelatin to harden).

When mixture is cooled, fold egg white mixture into egg yolk mixture. Pour filling into graham cracker crust and refrigerate 2 to 5 hours before serving.

# Pineapple Super-Pie

*Be sure to allow ample time for chilling.*

> 2 packages (8 ounces each) cream cheese
> 3 eggs
> ¾ cup sugar
> 1 teaspoon vanilla extract
> 1 Graham Cracker Crust (see page 207)
> 2 cans (20.5 ounces each) pineapple tidbits, some juice reserved
> ½ teaspoon unflavored gelatin

Preheat oven to 350 degrees. Using an electric mixer on medium speed, beat cream cheese, eggs, sugar, and vanilla extract. Pour mixture into pie crust. Bake 30 minutes or until it bounces back if touched with a fingertip. Place on a rack to cool.

Meanwhile, drain pineapple chunks, reserving ½ cup juice. Heat the pineapple juice in a saucepan over medium heat, and stir in gelatin until dissolved. Let cool.

Lay pineapple chunks in rows on pie. Cover with the gelatin glaze. Refrigerate 4 to 5 hours.

# Pumpkin Pie

1 cup sugar

1½ cups canned pumpkin or
mashed cooked pumpkin

1⅔ cups evaporated milk

2 eggs

1½ teaspoons cinnamon

½ teaspoon salt

½ teaspoon nutmeg

½ teaspoon powdered ginger

½ teaspoon allspice

½ teaspoon cloves

1 Pie Crust recipe (see page 207), bottom crust only,
pressed into a 9-inch pie plate

Preheat oven to 425 degrees. Using an electric mixer or a whisk, combine all ingredients except crust in a large bowl until smooth. Pour filling into unbaked pie shell. Bake for 15 minutes at 425 degrees, then lower temperature to 350 degrees and continue baking about 35 minutes or until custard is firm.

# Rhubarb Pie

*We ate rhubarb in sauce, in cake and pudding, and in several kinds of pie. The red stalks grew wild in the side yard.*

> Pie Crust recipe (see page 207)
> 5 cups diced or sliced young rhubarb,
>     unpeeled (if using older, "woodier"
>     rhubarb, peel before using)
> 1¼–2 cups sugar, to taste
> ¼ cup flour
> 1–2 tablespoons butter
> 1 teaspoon grated orange rind or lemon rind

Put rhubarb pieces in a large bowl. Sprinkle all of the remaining ingredients over the rhubarb, stir gently, and let stand for 15 minutes. Preheat oven to 400 degrees. Put 1 pie crust into a 9-inch pie plate.

Put the fruit mixture into the bottom pie crust and dot with 1 to 2 tablespoons of butter. Cover the filling with the second crust and seal the edges. With a sharp knife, cut decorative slits in the top crust. Bake 10 minutes.

Reduce the heat to 350 degrees and bake until the crust is golden brown and you can see the filling bubbling, 40 to 45 minutes longer.

# Puddings and Porridges

*Rødgrøt med Flote* (Red Fruit Pudding)

*Rømmegrøt* (Sour Cream Porridge)

*Tante* Synva's *Rømmegrøt* (Sour Cream Porridge)

Rød Saus (Red Sauce)

Strawberry Mousse

Eddie's Chocolate Mousse

Apple Cream Salad Dessert

# *Rødgrøt med Flote* (Red Fruit Pudding)

*This is the pudding that Erik and Quinn loved so much, and after eating it they enjoyed sticking out their red tongues. Our father asked the grocery store to stock Junket Danish Pudding, but we can no longer find Junket Danish Pudding or any other brand in the grocery store. Luckily, this recipe doesn't take too long to prepare.*

*If fresh fruit is unavailable, use canned or frozen raspberries and currants. Don't forget to allow enough time for the pudding to chill and set. Serves 5 to 6, with sweetened whipped cream.*

1 cup fresh red currants
1 cup red raspberries
1 cup sugar
⅛ teaspoon salt
1 stick cinnamon
1 cup water, divided
3 tablespoons potato flour or cornstarch

Combine fruit, sugar, salt, and cinnamon with ½ cup water and cook in a covered pan over medium-high heat for 15 to 20 minutes. Allow mixture to cool, then strain fruit carefully to remove the seeds, reserving juice. Return juice to heat. In a separate bowl, stir remaining ½ cup water into the potato flour or cornstarch to make a smooth paste. Add paste to the hot juice and stir constantly until the pudding is clear and thick. Pour into sherbet glasses or a glass bowl and allow to chill thoroughly.

# *Rømmegrøt* (Sour Cream Porridge)

*On my first trip to Norway in 1963, I was on the train from Oslo to Trondheim when the train stopped in Roros. As soon as we pulled into the station, everyone dashed off. Puzzled, I sat alone on the train until all the passengers returned. Later, I found out everyone had run off to get a bowl of rømmegrøt.*

*During that trip, we spent some time at Tante Ingeborg's great estate farmhouse at Leangen Gård, relaxing in the big farm kitchen. Maria, the housekeeper and cook for Tante Ingeborg, made us rømmegrøt—like my mother, she made it from scratch and not from a mix—and we all got to take turns stirring the cream as it cooked until the butter rose up into a pool at the top. When it was done, we sat around that huge wooden farm table, eating great bowls of rømmegrøt with a butter island from the reserved butter, fruit sauce, and a cold berry saft (fruit juice and simple syrup mixture) to drink, as happy as could be.  —Irene*

> 1 quart fresh cream, slightly sour,
>     or 1 quart buttermilk
> 3 pints whole milk
> 2 cups flour
> 2 tablespoons sugar
> 1 scant teaspoon salt
> Sprinkle of cinnamon

Boil cream or buttermilk in a double boiler over medium heat until butterfat floats to the top. Stir frequently. Pour off the butter and set the cream aside.

In the top of a double boiler, bring milk to a boil and then simmer over medium heat until butterfat rises to the top. Meanwhile, in a bowl, mix flour, sugar, and salt with enough water to make a paste. Add paste to simmering milk and blend well. Stir together milk mixture and cream, heat through, and serve piping hot in soup bowls, with a sprinkle of cinnamon on top and an island of reserved butter in each bowl. (If not enough butter rose to the top, you can melt additional butter and use that to put a small eye [øye] of butter into the middle of the bowl of *rømmegrøt*.)

## *Tante Synva's Rømmegrøt* (Sour Cream Porridge)

*Most people won't have access to fresh raw cream, but, for the sake of posterity, here is how our Tante Synva made rømmegrøt. She told me these directions on one of our visits to Walker, Minnesota.* —Irene

Keep 1 quart of fresh cream right from the cow until it turns a little sour. *Tante* Synva always said it was no good if the milk or cream was homogenized. Boil cream in a double boiler over medium heat, stirring frequently, until all the butter comes to the top. Pour the butter off and save for another use. Set aside the cream. Combine 2 cups flour with just enough water to make a paste. In a new pan over the double boiler, combine 3 pints of whole milk, flour paste, 2 tablespoons of sugar, and a scant teaspoon salt. Boil, stirring with a whisk, until the flour mixture is thoroughly combined and smooth. Stir the flour-milk mixture into the reserved cooked cream slowly, a little at a time. Serve hot, with a little cinnamon or crushed zwieback on top, a little of the reserved butter, and a cup of milk to pour over it. I like to drink a raspberry saft with this.

## *Rød Saus* (Red Sauce)

*Serve this vivid sauce with rømmegrøt, either poured on top or in a bowl on the side.*

> 1 cup tart red fruit juice, such as raspberry, cherry,
>     loganberry, or plum, freshly squeezed or preserved
> ⅔ cup water
> Sugar to taste
> 1 tablespoon potato flour, dissolved in 1 tablespoon cold water
> ½ teaspoon lemon juice or 1 teaspoon vanilla extract

In a small saucepan over high heat, mix juice with water and bring to a boil. Add sugar to taste. Stir in potato flour mixture, bring to a boil, then remove from heat to thicken and cool. When sauce has slightly cooled, add lemon juice or vanilla extract and serve.

# Strawberry Mousse

*Allow time for the strawberries to juice and several hours for the mousse to chill. Serves 8.*

> 1 pint strawberries
> 1 cup sugar
> 1 envelope (.25 ounce) strawberry gelatin
> 1 pint vanilla ice cream
> ½ cup coconut flakes
> ½ cup pecans, chopped fine

Special equipment: 4-cup mold

In a bowl, toss strawberries and sugar and let stand at room temperature 1 hour, tossing occasionally.

Drain berries, reserving juice, and add sufficient water to strawberry juice to make 1 cup. In a saucepan, bring juice to boil and pour into a large bowl over gelatin. Stir until gelatin is dissolved. Spoon ice cream into hot gelatin mixture and stir until melted. Let cool.

When the gelatin mixture is partially thickened, whip it with either a wire whisk or an electric hand mixer until completely smooth. Fold in strawberries, coconut, and pecans. (You can also reserve some of the berries and arrange them in an artful fashion in the bottom of the 4-cup mold before pouring the gelatin mixture over them.) Pour the gelatin into the mold and let chill in the refrigerator about 4 hours or until firm.

# Eddie's Chocolate Mousse

*Eddie's chocolate mousse was so delicious and popular that he always doubled the recipe. This version serves about 12 people.*

12 ounces semisweet chocolate chips
10 tablespoons butter
Two shakes of salt
8 eggs, separated
⅓–½ cup sugar
4 tablespoons vanilla extract
Chocolate sprinkles or chocolate curls

Melt the chocolate chips and butter in a double boiler, stirring with a wooden spoon. Stir in salt.

In a large bowl, beat the 8 egg whites with an electric mixer until stiff peaks form. Depending on how sweet you like it (or your weight), beat in ⅓ to ½ cup sugar. Refrigerate egg white mixture while you prepare the chocolate and egg yolks.

One at a time, stir egg yolks into the chocolate-butter mixture over the double boiler. Stir in vanilla extract. Continue stirring and cooking until very smooth. Chill in the refrigerator for about 10 minutes.

Thoroughly fold egg whites into the chocolate mixture. Refrigerate the completed mousse for 2 to 3 hours. Serve sprinkled with chocolate sprinkles or chocolate curls.

# Apple Cream Salad Dessert

*Prepare this recipe several hours or one day ahead.*

> 4 large apples, peeled and diced
> 1 can (20 ounces) sliced pineapple,
>     drained and juice reserved, coarsely chopped
> 8 large marshmallows, cut in half
> 3 tablespoons unsalted butter
> 3 tablespoons flour
> 1½ tablespoons sugar
> 1 can (14 ounces) sweetened condensed milk

Lay half the apples in a bowl, then layer half the pineapple pieces over the apples. Repeat, finishing with pineapple. Top with marshmallow halves.

Melt butter in a pan, add flour and sugar, and mix well. Add reserved pineapple juice and sweetened condensed milk. Boil until thick. Pour dressing over fruit and refrigerate overnight or until firm.

# Candies

# CANDIED CITRUS PEEL

Gudrun used every part of a fruit or vegetable to make something delicious. When we had good citrus fruit, she always peeled them carefully and reserved the peels. She usually cut the peel in long, narrow strips, or sometimes other shapes, and covered them with glacé or dipped them in melted chocolate. And how delicious that was.

## Candied Orange Peel

*This recipe works equally well for lemons and oranges. You may cut the peel in larger pieces (such as halves or quarters) if you allow a longer cooking time in the syrup.*

> 4 large navel oranges
> Sugar
> Cold water
> Additional sugar for garnish

Have a buttered platter ready. Peel oranges and cut the rinds into pieces of uniform size, about 1 inch long and ¼ inch wide. Measure the peel in a measuring cup and set aside an equal amount of sugar.

Place peel in a saucepan. Cover with cold water and bring almost to the boiling point, but do not boil. Pour off the scalding water and repeat this process two more times, then drain the peel.

Add sugar, cover with cold water, and boil until no syrup shows in the saucepan when it is tipped. Spread peels on buttered platter and roll them in sugar when partially cooled. Dry thoroughly before packing in airtight containers.

# Candied Grapefruit Peel

*Grapefruit peel requires a longer scalding than lemon or orange peel.*
*Be sure to cut the white pith off of the peel.*

> 1 large grapefruit
> Cold water
> Sugar
> A few drops almond extract (optional)

Wash and peel the grapefruit. Cut the rind into pieces ½ inch wide and 1 inch long. Measure peel and set aside 1 cup of sugar for each cup of peel.

Place peel in a saucepan, cover with cold water, and bring to a boil. Boil for 5 minutes. Drain, fill with fresh water, and bring to a boil again. Repeat. Boil the rind in the fourth change of water until tender, then drain and place in a fifth change of water, adding almond extract, if using, and the sugar. Boil the grapefruit rind until the liquid becomes a thick syrup. Drain grapefruit peel and roll in sugar.

# Glacéed Fruits and Nuts

*These were festive treats during holiday times.*

> 2 cups sugar
> 1 cup water
> Pinch of cream of tartar
> 1 pound fresh fruit or shelled nuts,
>     such as grapes, plums, strawberries,
>     walnuts, or almonds

Special equipment: candy thermometer, paper cases for candy

Butter two baking pans and set aside. Heat a pan of water to boiling and keep hot.

Place sugar and water in a separate saucepan and cook, stirring, until sugar is dissolved. Add the cream of tartar and cook, without stirring, until a temperature of 290 degrees is reached on a thermometer (also known as the soft-crack stage, when a spoonful of syrup dropped in cold water cracks, but is still slightly pliable). As the syrup is cooking, without shaking the saucepan, use a spatula to scrape away any sugar crystals that may form on the sides of the pan.

When syrup reaches 290 degrees, remove from heat and set saucepan in pan of boiling water to prevent hardening. Using a toothpick for the fruit and a slotted spoon for the nuts, dip each fruit or nut, one at a time, into the hot syrup, taking care to cover the pieces completely. Lay candied pieces on buttered pans in a cool place to let them dry and harden. If the first dipping is not successful (the sugar syrup did not completely cover the item, or did not stick) repeat the dipping process. When glacéed fruit or nuts have dried and hardened, place each one in a paper case and keep in an airtight container.

# MARZIPAN CANDY

Marzipan ("almond bread") candy has been made in Europe for centuries. There is a wide variation in recipes, but making marzipan can be as simple as combining equal parts almond paste and vanilla fondant. Gudrun made the marzipan into the shape of tiny fruits, flowers, and vegetables, all colored and decorated accordingly. These can be fashioned with the fingers and the simplest kitchen tools, or, for more elaborate and professional-looking confections, with special molds made of metal or mounted in plaster of Paris. Gudrun fashioned these small fruits and vegetable shapes with her hands. After shaping and drying, marzipans may also be coated with melted fondant, melted chocolate, glacé syrup, colored sugar, or tinted coconut.

Gudrun always blanched and chopped her own almonds into a fine flourlike powder for making marzipan candy (or *kransekaker*, *fyrstekake*, *sandbakkels*, or almond cake). Whenever she needed freshly ground almonds, Eddie and I, who loved to be in the kitchen when our mother was making something special, would have a little job to do. We would sit at the kitchen table and get all of the brown skin off the almonds after she had blanched them.

Once our mother had made the almond paste, she would use her fingers to make lifelike strawberries, potatoes, bananas, kiwis, oranges, lemons, and other fruits and vegetables. She tinted her own ultrafine sugars with food coloring to resemble the right colors, and she used cloves and plastic strawberry stems for decoration. Gudrun's marzipan candy was just right, not too sweet like so many of the store-bought marzipan candies from famous European candy makers. It tasted just like almonds. The consistency was smooth, sometimes a little grainy—so you knew you were eating the real thing.

## BLANCHING AND CHOPPING ALMONDS

First Gudrun placed shelled almonds in a saucepan. She covered them with cold water, brought them to a boil, then removed them from heat. She'd drain the almonds, run cold water over them, and turn them out onto a coarse cloth. Eddie and I would use the cloth to rub off the outer brown skin.

The next step was to put the nuts in the big curved wooden bowl my mother used for chopping nuts and vegetables. With the chopper—a curved double-bladed knife with a handle—I would chop and chop and chop. The almonds still looked fairly coarse when I finished. But then our mother would start. With her strong arms she would chop until soon the nuts were as fine as sand or flour.

Now people grind the blanched almonds with a blender or food processor or better yet a special almond grinder. That often does not get the same consistency throughout, but it does work. You simply have to be careful not to grind them too much. —Irene

## MAKING MARZIPAN GOODIES

With a good, smooth marzipan paste, a variety of food colorings, and a bit of creativity, it is possible to make almost any kind of vegetable, fruit, or flower. Among the simplest to make are carrots, green beans, peas in the pod, pumpkins, apples, oranges, bananas, rosebuds, violets, and Easter lilies. Here are instructions for a few more complicated shapes.

**Potatoes:** Shape small pieces of uncolored marzipan like potatoes. Use a toothpick or small skewer to make dents for the eyes. Roll in cocoa powder, cinnamon, or cinnamon sugar.

**Pears:** Mold yellow-tinted marzipan in the shape of a small pear, making the stem and blossom ends with cloves. With a brush, apply diluted red food coloring to one side of the pear (optional).

**Strawberries:** Dip marzipan strawberries in beaten egg white and then roll in red tinted sugar. Tuck green stem and leaf paper hulls into the tops and use a toothpick to poke dents to resemble seeds.

**Stuffed fruits:** Stuff glacéed cherries, dates, prunes, figs, and raisins with bits of marzipan, adding a decorative finish if desired.

**Marzipan bars:** Roll out a piece of colored marzipan and cover with a layer of fondant. Top with another layer of marzipan and cut into bars. A glacé or melted chocolate covering may be added when the bars are dried.

**Harlequin balls:** Roll two colored pieces of marzipan lightly between the palms and the colors will blend, making an attractive harlequin ball.

**Stuffed nuts:** Secure two pecan or walnut halves with a small piece of tinted marzipan and cover with glacé syrup.

# Easy Marzipan Candy

8 ounces almond paste
6 ounces confectioners' sugar
2 ounces light corn syrup
⅔ cup marshmallow crème
   or melted marshmallow

Combine all ingredients in a food processor until blended. Immediately after blending, and before the mixture dries too much, form into desired shapes. This can be too sweet, so go easy on added sugar.

# Simple Cooked Marzipan

*If you use molds, do not wash them before using for the first time; instead lightly brush them with olive oil and wipe them with a soft cloth. There is no need to buy molds, however; Gudrun fashioned her marzipan into fruits and vegetables using her hands.*

3 cups sugar
1 cup water
5 cups ground almonds
1 teaspoon flavoring extract such as vanilla
   extract or lemon extract, or more to taste
Food coloring

Dissolve the sugar in the water in a saucepan over medium heat. Add the almonds. Cook, stirring constantly, until the mass will not adhere to the pan. Remove pan from heat and turn out paste onto a clean marble slab, enamel tabletop, or baking sheet. Knead until smooth, adding flavoring extract and coloring while mixture is still warm. Shape as desired. Store in an airtight container.

# Uncooked Marzipan

*Allow a few hours for the marzipan to rest before forming into shapes.*

½ cup confectioners' sugar
½ cup granulated sugar
2 cups ground almonds
2 egg whites
1 teaspoon flavoring extract, such as vanilla
extract or lemon extract, or more to taste
Food coloring

Sift the sugars together. Add the almonds and mix well. In a separate bowl, beat the egg whites with an electric mixer until frothy, then blend into the sugar and almond mixture. Add flavoring extract and coloring and blend well.

Turn mixture out onto a clean marble slab, enamel tabletop, or baking sheet and knead until smooth (before kneading, the texture will be grainy). If paste is not stiff enough to hold a shape, add a little more sugar.

Allow the mixture to stand for a few hours, then press small pieces of it into molds, form into dainty shapes, or roll out and cut with small cutters. This marzipan should be served and eaten within a few weeks, as it does not keep well for any length of time.

# Make Up and Use Later Marzipan

*You can purchase flavored fondant and glucose (a type of corn syrup) in specialty kitchen supply stores.*

4 cups ground almonds
1¼ pounds flavored fondant
4 cups sugar
2 cups water
1 tablespoon glucose
1 teaspoon flavoring extract, such as vanilla
    extract or lemon extract, or more to taste
Food coloring

**Special equipment: candy thermometer**

Work the ground almonds into the fondant with a wooden spoon, blending thoroughly.

Place the sugar and water in a saucepan and heat slowly until sugar dissolves. Add the glucose and boil, without stirring, until mixture reaches 250 degrees on a candy thermometer or until a drop forms a hard ball in cold water. Quickly add the sugar syrup to the fondant-almond mixture and stir until the mixture begins to harden. Then turn out onto a clean, hard surface and knead until smooth. Add flavoring extract and coloring while dough is still warm.

This marzipan keeps well if wrapped first in waxed paper, then in a clean cloth, and stored in an airtight box. If it hardens before you want to use it, add a few drops of lukewarm water and mix well.

# Pickles and Preserves

# CANNING INSTRUCTIONS

I have vivid memories of being in the kitchen with my mother when she was canning anything. She tended strawberries in barrels. When peaches were in season, she bought a barrel and pickled them. She pickled the crab apples that grew on the tree in the back yard, picked and canned raspberries for jam, and saved watermelon rinds for making watermelon pickles. I would stir and stir the large pot in the kitchen. My mother would carefully take the boiled, sterilized jars and lids out of the large canning pot and turn them upside down, being careful so as not to contaminate the sterilized jars. Of course she was making bread at the same time, and the aromas together were tantalizing. We would get some of the jam on that bread before it was poured into the canning jar and before the melted canning wax was poured on top. Then after it all cooled, we would carry the jars to the basement to put on the shelves that our dad had made for home canned goods, to wait for the long cold winter.

The recipes included here use the methods Gudrun followed. However, readers should instruct themselves on canning techniques and food safety issues before attempting to can foods at home. Luckily, there are myriad books available that offer detailed instructions for canning and preserving food safely. Another good source for instructions and recipes is your local county extension agent.  —Irene

## Sweet Pickled Watermelon

*When we had watermelon, Gudrun cut off the green part, and after we ate the watermelon, she kept the white rind and made watermelon pickles that we enjoyed all year as a condiment. You can purchase mixed pickling spices in most grocery stores. The rinds will need to soak overnight before pickling.*

> 2 pounds watermelon rind
> ¼ cup salt to 1 quart water
> 1 pint vinegar diluted with 1 pint water

4 cups sugar

¼ cup mixed pickle spices, tied in cheesecloth bag

Special equipment: 12 sterilized jars and lids, pressure cooker, cheesecloth

Pare rind, leaving some of the red flesh, and cut into small strips or squares. Soak overnight in salt water, using ratio above.

Drain watermelon rind, add fresh water, and boil about 20 minutes, until tender enough that a fork punctures the fruit easily but it is still slightly crisp. Drain rind and set aside.

Boil vinegar, water, and sugar to make a syrup. Add the bag of spices and the watermelon rind. Boil slowly until liquid is clear, 5 to 10 minutes. Remove spice bag and pour rind and hot liquid into airtight sterile jars. Follow manufacturer's directions to seal jars in a pressure cooker for 20 minutes.

# Watermelon Rind Preserves I

*This recipe also works well with unripe cantaloupe.*

4 cups ½-inch cubes peeled underripe watermelon rind,
    with plenty of the firm, red pulp

3 cups sugar

3 lemons, or 2 oranges and 1 lemon, sliced thin and seeded

Grated pineapple (optional)

Special equipment: 12 sterilized jars and lids, pressure cooker

Combine melon rind, sugar, and lemon slices in a pot and boil slowly for about 2 hours, until the rind is clear and the juice is thick. If desired, when nearly done add a small can of grated pineapple and cook 15 minutes longer. Place preserves in airtight jars. Follow manufacturer's directions to seal jars in a pressure cooker for 20 minutes.

# Watermelon Rind Preserves II

*These preserves need several weeks to rest before they are ready to eat.*

> 7 pounds watermelon rind
> 1 teaspoon lump alum
> ½ teaspoon salt
> 5 pounds sugar, white and light brown,
>     mixed (approximately a 50-50 ratio)
> 1 quart vinegar mixed with 1 pint of water
> 6 sticks cinnamon
> 1 tablespoon cloves

Special equipment: 12 sterilized jars and lids, pressure cooker

Pare rind and cut into strips. Boil in a large pot of water with alum and salt until tender and clear, about 20 minutes. Drain. Chill in cold water. Dry rind on a cloth.

Place sugar, vinegar, and water in a pot and boil to a light syrup. Add spices and melon rind. Boil until clear. Remove spices. Pour preserves into airtight jars and seal. Follow manufacturer's directions to seal jars in a pressure cooker for 20 minutes. Let this stand for 4 weeks before eating.

# Pickled Crab Apples

*We had a crab apple tree in our yard to provide fruit for this sweet-sour preserve.*

6 pounds crab apples, whole, unpeeled
1 quart cider vinegar
2 cups sugar
1 tablespoon cloves, 2 cinnamon sticks,
    and 1 tablespoon fresh chopped ginger,
    tied in cheesecloth bag

Special equipment: 12 sterilized jars and lids, pressure cooker, cheesecloth

Wash the crab apples and steam them in a colander over boiling water until soft. Place fruit in a large saucepan with vinegar, sugar, and spices. Bring slowly to a boil and cook gently about 20 minutes. Pour into sterilized jars and seal. Follow manufacturer's directions to seal jars in a pressure cooker.

# ACKNOWLEDGMENTS

We are grateful to the elders and storytellers in our family: the late Liv "Tuty" Brakke Herstgaard (whom we interviewed about our family history in 2007, shortly before she passed on at ninety-one years of age), the late *Tante* Ragnhild Thue Hoye (the longest surviving of the Thue girls, who videotaped her story of the Thues before her death at age ninety-seven), and to Gudrun and Irving Sandvold and all of our ancestors for giving us the stories to tell and the meals to go with them.

We give thanks to our relatives near and far for their input and support in helping us piece together the puzzle of the Thue family's history, including Karen Sandvold, Erik Sandvold, Ingeborg Stensrud, Bjorg Oie, Dale Erik Sandvold, and Adelaide Brakke. Thank you, also, to friends in Fort Atkinson, Wisconsin, and University of Wisconsin friends and classmates who shared stories about Gudrun.

Thank you to all of the professionals at the Wisconsin Historical Society Press, including Kate Thompson and Michelle Wildgen, for their patience and expertise in editing, and Dee Grimsrud, whose priceless historical and genealogical research has become a family treasure. Also, thanks to Astrid Karlsen Scott, who took the time to give some advice and encouragement to Ingeborg when she was looking to publish.

And last but not least, thanks to our top taste-testers, Lars H. Hydle, Lars S. Hydle, and LaVar Baugh.

# SOURCES FOR NORWEGIAN COOKING IMPLEMENTS AND FOODS

**Ingebretsen's Scandinavian Gifts and Foods**
1601 East Lake Street
Minneapolis, MN 55407
612-729-9333 or 800-279-9333
www.ingebretsens.com
Ingebretsen's is an online source of Scandinavian food, crafts, cookware, needlework, and clothing.

**Jacobs of Willmar, Inc.**
2166 Sixty-sixth Avenue NE
Willmar, MN 56201
800-891-7594
This store carries pastry boards, pastry board cloth covers, electric griddles, rolling pin cloth covers, and *lefse* turning sticks. Order more than one pastry board and rolling pin cover; that way, if the dough is sticking to the pastry board or rolling pin, you can change them and keep going.

# GLOSSARY

**berlinerkranser:** "Berlin wreaths," or small wreath-shaped cookies frequently made at Christmas

**blodklubb:** dumplings made with blood

**bløtkake:** layer cake frosted with whipped cream and filled with whipped cream or custard, usually with fresh berries in the filling or topping. Gudrun often used a rum custard filling.

**bonde ost:** "farmer cheese"; a cylinder-shaped, firm, mild, cow's milk cheese, sometimes with cumin or caraway seeds, that is briefly brined and ripened for six to eight weeks

**brunost:** "brown cheese," also called *gjetost*, or caramelized goat cheese

**far i kal:** lamb in cabbage; a very popular Norwegian dish

**fattigmanns:** "poor man" cookies; the diamond-shaped cookie is deep-fried and sprinkled with confectioners' sugar.

**finnan haddie:** smoked haddock

**fiskeboller:** small, dumpling-like fish balls, made with cod or other firm white fish, homemade or available in cans

**flatbrød:** unleavened bread often made with rye flour. We ate this daily, with meals and coffee—Gudrun always said that a few pieces of *flatbrød* would add years to your life.

**frokost:** breakfast

**fyrstekake:** "prince's cake," a special-occasion cake that has a delicious almond macaroon filling and often a layer of raspberry jam. Gudrun's nephew Sten Stensrud and his wife, Anne Lise, often mailed her a *fyrstekake* in a beautiful round tin for Christmas.

**fyrstekake med epler:** prince's cake with apples

**gammalost:** "old cheese." Light gold in color and quite strong-smelling, *gammalost* is best sliced thin and served on dark bread, *flatbrød*, or even *lefse*. Irving loved *gammalost*, so Gudrun kept it in its own tightly closed container—on the back porch. *Gammalost* is often spelled *gammelost* and *gamelost*, likely due to different dialects.

**gjetost:** goat cheese. See *brunost*

**gravlaks:** "buried salmon," or salmon cured in salt, sugar, and dill. Gudrun often served *gravlaks* with creamed diced potatoes, mustard sauce, cucumber salad, *flatbrød*, and lemon wedges.

**julaften:** Christmas Eve

**juledag:** Christmas Day

**julekake:** "Christmas cake"; a sweet bread flavored with citron, raisins, and cardamom

**kaffe bord er dekket:** Literally, "Coffee table is filled," meaning the food is laid out and ready for the guest to eat

**klubb:** dumplings. Gudrun usually made potato dumplings, but they also may be made with flour, and they usually have a piece of salt pork in the center.

**koldtbord:** "cold table," equivalent of the cold food selections of the *smörgåsbord*; a meal served buffet-style with multiple dishes

**kransekake:** "ring cake," usually eaten on special occasions such as birthdays, weddings, baptisms, Christmas, or New Year's Eve. *Kransekake* is made of rings of almond-flour cake, layered in a pyramid, and decorated with white frosting, Norwegian flags, and some mementos for the occasion.

**kringle:** "ring" or "circle"; a Norwegian oval-shaped pastry, iced and filled with jam, fruit, or nuts

**krumkake:** a patterned crisp cookie cooked in a two-sided flat iron and flavored with cardamom. *Krumkake* are usually rolled into cones, but Gudrun sometimes shaped the warm cookie into a cup and filled it with whipped cream and fresh berries.

**lapskaus:** a variation of beef stew often made with gravy. Gudrun diced the beef and potatoes into very tiny pieces and served it with cooked carrots, *flatbrød*, and cucumber salad.

**lefse:** soft, thin, griddled Norwegian flatbread. The dough is often made with cooked potatoes that have been mashed or riced. Today many people make it with instant potato buds.

**lutefisk:** dried cod treated with lye. Gudrun said it was buried in the ground and dug up when one wanted to eat it.

**mat:** food

**moster:** maternal aunt

**napoleonskake:** "Napoleon cake," made of two or more layers of puff pastry, filled with whipped cream and vanilla and rum custards and iced on top

**nattmat:** "night meal" or midnight snack

**nøkkelost:** "key cheese," a semihard cow's milk cheese flavored with cumin and caraway

**ost:** cheese

**ostehøvel:** cheese slicer

**pariser:** an open-face sandwich consisting of buttered bread topped with minced beef, egg yolk, breadcrumbs, grated onions, seasoning such as nutmeg and a little pepper, and capers

**ribbe:** rib pork chops, a Norwegian Christmas specialty

**rømmegrøt:** sour cream porridge. Nowadays *rømmegrøt* is often made with cream instead of sour cream.

**sandbakkels:** "sand tarts" or almond cookies baked in fluted, circular or rectangular molds to look like miniature pie crusts

**selskap:** party, celebration, or get-together. A *familie selskap* is a family party.

**sillsallad:** herring salad

**smørbrød:** open-faced sandwich consisting of a single slice of bread with one or more food items on top, usually eaten with knife and fork

**smörgåsbord:** literally "bread and butter table"; a Scandinavian buffet featuring hot and cold dishes. In Norway, when the dishes are a mixture of cold dishes, meats, breads, salads, and fish, it is called *koldtbord*.

**spekemat:** salt-cured meat

**surkål:** sweet and sour sliced, cooked cabbage with caraway seeds, similar to sauerkraut

**tante:** aunt

**troll:** a creature from Scandinavian folklore that lives in caves or hills

**tytebaer:** lingonberry, a tart red berry similar to a smaller, juicier cranberry

**uff dah:** a common Scandinavian expression, similar to a sigh of fatigue, disgust, or sensory overload. Often the equivalent of "Good grief" or "Oh, boy."

**Vær så god:** Literally "Be so good," but can mean almost anything, depending on the context, such as "Have a seat," "Can I help you?" or "Help yourself at the table."

# BIBLIOGRAPHY

*Berolzheimer, Ruth. *The Candy Book: Everything You Need to Know about Making . . . Fondant Candies; Chocolate Candies; Fudges; Caramels; Divinities and Nougats; Taffies and Kisses; Brittles and Hard Candies; Uncooked Candies; Maple Candies; Coconut Candies; Marzipans; Glacéed Fruits and Nuts.* Chicago: Consolidated Book Publishers Inc., 1941.

Brown, Dale, and the editors of Time Life Books. *The Cooking of Scandinavia.* New York: Time Life Books, 1968.

*Cookbook Committee, Ladies Aid Society. *Cook Book of Tested Recipes.* Minneapolis, MN: Norwegian Lutheran Memorial Church (Mindekirken), The Cookbook Committee, undated.

Haugen, Einar. *Beginning Norwegian, A Grammar and Reader,* 3rd ed. London: George G. Harrap and Co., Ltd., 1937; reprinted 1961.

Haugen, Einar, and Kenneth G. Chapman. *Spoken Norwegian,* rev. ed. New York: Holt Rinehart and Winston, 1964.

*Kander, Lizzie S. *The Settlement Cook Book: The Way to a Man's Heart.* Milwaukee: J. H. Yewdale and Sons Co., 1901.

*Landstad-Jensen, M. *Cook Book of Norwegian Recipes.* Brooklyn, NY: Norwegian News Company, 1947.

Lovoll, Odd S. *The Promise of America: A History of the Norwegian-American People,* rev. ed.Minneapolis University of Minnesota Press, 1999.

Myhre, Helen, and Mona Vold. *Farm Recipes and Food Secrets from the Norske Nook.* Madison: University of Wisconsin Press, 2001.

Scott, Astrid Karlsen. *Ekte Norsk Mat.* Olympia, WA: Nordic Adventures, 1995.

Tufford, Julia Peterson. *Scandinavian Recipes Including the Smorgasbord.* Minneapolis: self-published, 1958; first copyright 1940.

\* *The cookbooks noted with an asterisk belonged to Gudrun.*

# INDEX

# ABOUT THE AUTHORS

**Irene Sandvold** grew up in Fort Atkinson, Wisconsin, and graduated from the University of Wisconsin School of Nursing in 1960. She went on to become a doctor of public health, a public health nurse, and a certified nurse-midwife and is a leader in her field. To those who know her, she is an extraordinary chef and hostess in the tradition of her mother, Gudrun. She and her husband, Lars H. Hydle, raised their two children, Lars and Ingeborg, in Washington, D.C.

Irene's daughter, **Ingeborg Hydle Baugh**, is a freelance writer with a background in finance, a master's in Business Administration, and bachelor's in Economics. After working for nearly a decade in finance, she decided to focus entirely on writing. She aspires to carry on the traditions of her mother and grandmother but always prefers her mother's cooking to her own. She lives in Washington, D.C., with her husband, LaVar Baugh.

Like his sister, Irene, **Edward Sandvold** graduated from the University of Wisconsin, as did his wife, Karen. Eddie and Karen raised their sons, Erik and Quinn, in Boulder, Colorado, where Eddie founded a publishing company. His love of food and cooking began in his mother's kitchen, where, at about age seven, he created his own cookbook entirely devoted to Gudrun's chocolate desserts. He channeled her joy and excitement into every dish and delighted in replicating the unique tastes and flavors of her food. He passed away in 2005.

Eddie's son **Quinn Sandvold** has been a lifelong cook in the tradition of his father and grandmother. He is a designer for snowboarding gear and equipment and former national amateur snowboard champion, professional snowboarder, and fly fishing guide. He lives in Longmont, Colorado, and has spent years trying to make his gravy taste like Gudrun's.